DRINKING WITH THE DEMOCRATS

DRINKING

with the

DEMOCRATS

THE PARTY ANIMAL'S HISTORY OF LIBERAL LIBATIONS

MARK WILL-WEBER

REGNERY
HISTORY
Washington, D.C.

Regnery History™ is a trademark of Salem Communications Holding Corporation
Regnery® is a registered trademark and its colophon is a trademark of Salem Communications Holding Corporation

ISBN: 978-1-68451-495-3
Library of Congress Control Number: 2016020396

Cataloging-in-Publication data on file with the Library of Congress

Published in the United States by
Regnery History, an Imprint of
Regnery Publishing
A Division of Salem Media Group
Washington, D.C.
www.RegneryHistory.com

Manufactured in the United States of America

10 9 8 7 6 5 4 3 2 1

Book interior design: Jason Sunde

Books are available in quantity for promotional or premium use.
For information on discounts and terms, please visit our website:
www.Regnery.com.

CONTENTS

★ THE PRESIDENTS ★

INTRODUCTION

CHEERS! You hold in your hands the best way to celebrate the history of our great nation, with rich stories of White House drinking and a bevy of cocktail recipes to boot! So get out your cocktail shaker, stock up on your best mixers, and prepare to bend an elbow in honor of your favorite Democrats and their drinks.

Author Mark Will-Weber has plumbed the archives for the best stories about presidential drinking. He has unearthed hundreds of anecdotes, fun facts, and legends covering more than two and a quarter centuries.

I hope you enjoy perusing this book to learn about the original party animals. Inside, you'll discover Andrew Jackson's hillbilly supporters trashing the Executive Mansion, you'll read about which Democrats used the sauce to buy votes, and you'll be shocked to find out how LBJ recklessly drinking and driving around his sprawling Texas ranch.

And for each president, a cocktail recipe is provided so you can play along at home. Some of the recipes are that president's actual favorite cocktail, and others are contrivances based on that president's life or background. Sure, some could be called a bit of a stretch, but they're all legitimate cocktails that you might like to give a shake.

We tried to keep it fun, so go ahead and read about the tippling POTUSes, and mix up a cocktail or two to shake things up. And while Democrats may only show moderation during the general election campaign, we recommend that you always drink in moderation.

Alex Novak
Publisher
Regnery History

A NOTE ABOUT
THE PARTIES

THIS BOOK is called *Drinking with the Democrats*. But not all of the presidents covered herein were actually Democrats. We didn't want to leave out some of the greatest and best-known early presidents; so, after careful thought, so we took liberties and drafted some of those early presidents into the Democratic ranks. Included as Democrats for the purposes of this book are Thomas Jefferson, who was a Democratic-Republican, as were James Madison, James Monroe, and John Quincy Adams. While it could be argued that Adams could easily be grouped with his father in the Republican camp, we decided to keep all the Democratic-Republicans together. Sometimes party lines are thicker than blood. The companion to this edition is called *Drinking with the Republicans*. In that book, we included the independent George Washington, along with Federalist John Adams, and Whigs Harrison, Tyler, Taylor, and Fillmore all with the Republicans.

THOMAS

JEFFERSON

★ 1801–1809 ★

"I AM NOW IN THE LAND OF CORN, WINE,
OIL AND SUNSHINE. WHAT MORE CAN A MAN
ASK OF HEAVEN?"

—Thomas Jefferson

FOUNDING FATHER OF WINE

H E DRAFTED THE Declaration of Independence, oversaw the Louisiana Purchase—which more than doubled the size of the country—and unleashed the fury of the U.S. Navy against the Barbary Coast pirates. But for connoisseurs of fine vintages, Thomas Jefferson will always be regarded as the First Father of Wine in the United States.

That is not to suggest that there wasn't wine present in America long before Jefferson; wine arrived virtually with the first Europeans. Jefferson, however, knew that truly wonderful wine—like art, literature, or architecture—could be something splendid and exhilarating. The "Sage of Monticello" had not used his time in France (1784–1788) solely in diplomatic toil. Always keen to pursue both his intellectual and sensual interests, Jefferson went to "walk about" for several weeks in southern France and the Italian Piedmont in 1787. He learned firsthand about European wine culture—from vine to wine cellar. By the time he returned to the States, Jefferson's wine expertise was quite likely second to none among his countrymen.

Jefferson's love of the best wines and his urge to share his bottles with his friends and guests greatly contributed to his precarious financial situation. Some years he spent thousands of dollars on wine alone. By the time of his death on July 4, 1826 (just hours before his former foe John Adams died in Massachusetts), the third president of the United States was on the brink of bankruptcy.

THE BANE OF WHISKEY

Unlike some American presidents who followed him, Thomas Jefferson was not a whiskey man; in fact, his zeal for wine was matched by his disdain for hard spirits. As he once wrote to a French acquaintance:

> It is an error to view a tax on that liquor [wine] as merely a tax against the rich. It is a prohibition of its use to the middling class of our citizens, and a condemnation of them to the poison of whiskey, which is desolating their houses. No nation is drunken where wine is cheap; and none sober, where the dearness of wine substitutes ardent spirits as the common beverage. It is, in truth, the only antidote to the bane of whiskey.

Although many of the prominent men of his day were proud whiskey drinkers, Jefferson must have witnessed how overindulgence in hard liquor was a shortcut to ruination. He was well aware that alcohol addiction shortened the promising lives of both the writer Thomas Paine and the intrepid explorer Meriwether Lewis. Closer to home, Jefferson's writings reveal that several of his skilled laborers at Monticello—specifically his blacksmith William Orr and cabinet-maker David Watson—

> No nation is drunken where wine is cheap....

drank whiskey to excess and sometimes missed days of work because of it. Besides having hangovers of their own, the drinking duo must have been a headache to Jefferson, though he apparently overlooked their flaws because of their talents.

WHAT WOULD TOM DRINK?

Jefferson became acquainted with wine well before he traveled to France. At the College of William and Mary, and later as a law student in Williamsburg, Jefferson was introduced to the stronger Madeira wines and, in fact, had kegs of it in his cellar at Monticello on the eve of the Revolution. (He also may have occasionally drunk some "arrack"—liquor distilled with sugarcane and something of a cousin of rum, minus the molasses.)

But his experience in France—sampling the best vintages from Dr. Ben Franklin's well-stocked Paris cellar, or from his growing circle of friends in the French aristocracy—gradually pushed him in another direction. His 1787 trip to vineyards in the south of France and northern Italy lifted Jefferson to a higher plateau in his "wine education," and it certainly qualified as some of the happiest days of his life. During this most pleasant trek, he wrote to his secretary, William Short:

> I am now in the land of corn, wine, oil and sunshine. What more can a man ask of heaven? If I should die at Paris I will beg of you to send my body here and have me exposed to the sun. I am sure it will bring me to life again.

As a halfhearted excuse to go on the trip, Jefferson journeyed to a French hot springs spa to help heal a badly injured wrist. But his daughter Martha wasn't completely buying that line. She teased her father, writing: "I am inclined to think that your voyage is rather for your pleasure than your health."

Jefferson's favorite wines appear to have been top-quality vintages of Bordeaux, Burgundy, and Sauterne. Jefferson also had a special fondness for white Hermitage, ordered it often, and once lauded it as "the first wine in the world without a single exception." And Jefferson drank wine the rest of his life. Writing to Dr. Vine Utley in March 1821, the seventy-six-year-old Jefferson (after learning that Dr. Benjamin Rush typically drank a glass and a half of Madeira wine each day) noted:

I double, however, the Doctor's glass and a half of wine, and treble it with a friend; but halve its effects by drinking the weak wines only. The ardent wines I cannot drink, nor do I use any ardent spirits in any form. Malt liquors and cider are my table drinks....

The glasses of wine always came after dinner, to stimulate conversation and camaraderie. Always keen on inventive flourishes, Jefferson had dumbwaiters on each side of the fireplace so that fresh wine could arrive straight from the cellar with minimal interruption—and emptied bottles could be dispatched downward.

TABLE TIPPLES

Jefferson had such an affinity for wine that it might be easy to overlook any other alcoholic beverages he enjoyed. But Jefferson served beer and hard apple cider as his "table" drinks at dinner. Prior to the Revolutionary War, Jefferson's wife, Martha, brewed some big batches of beer at Monticello—sometimes as much as fifteen to twenty gallons of "small" beer (which would have been low in alcohol) every several weeks. Martha added a little zip to its taste by including some hops. In later years, Jefferson brought in an experienced brewer named John Miller, a British soldier who stayed in America after the war. Miller taught the basics of brewing to Jefferson's kitchen slave, Peter Heming.

Although Jefferson is famous for his quotes on wine, he also gave a favorable nod to beer, noting: "Beer, if drunk in moderation, softens the temper, cheers the spirit, and promotes health." Jefferson longed to establish European vines at his homestead, but his attempts failed due to blight and bad weather. Virginia did produce bountiful apple crops, however, and good strong cider, like beer, was always plentiful at Monticello.

Visitors to Monticello sometimes commented that Jefferson looked younger than his years. He offset his appetites with vigorous walks and horseback rides around the estate, until bouts of rheumatism slowed him down in his last years. Tall and relatively athletic, the redheaded Jefferson held his years well, despite the gallons of alcohol (and abundance of food) at his disposal.

MIND ON THE WINE

Jefferson wrote often about wine. On April 8, 1817, for example, he began a letter to his friend James Monroe, who had just been inaugurated as the fifth president of the United States:

> I shall not waste your time in idle congratulations. You know my joy on the commitment of the helm of our government to your hands....
>
> I promised you, when I should have received and tried the wines I ordered from France and Italy, to give you a note....

Whereupon the Sage of Monticello charged on for several detailed paragraphs about some of the most celebrated vintages grown in Europe and where to buy them. President Monroe responded the next month by profusely thanking his mentor for his expertise on wine and even offering to expand his (Monroe's) order, just in case Jefferson wanted more wine for himself.

John Quincy Adams, on the other hand, wasn't enthused about the topic of vintages. In 1807, when Jefferson was still president, Adams was invited to dinner. In his diary entry, Adams—whose father had been one of Jefferson's rivals—yawningly penned: "There was, as usual, a dissertation upon wines. Not very edifying."

As for Jefferson, he even found wine a suitable simile for friendship itself. In an 1811 letter to Dr. Benjamin Rush, he wrote: "I find friendship to be like wine, raw when new, ripened with age, the true old man's milk and restorative cordial...."

THE DAMAGES

Jefferson was quite diligent about recording how much wine he bought and how much his guests consumed. He bought in very large quantities, but since he entertained almost constantly, the

WINE ON THE FOURTH OF JULY

TJ was a wine snob. He didn't care much for the hard stuff. He liked wine, and lots of it. But wine is often simply consumed in a glass. One doesn't require a recipe for that. However, the Declaration of Independence is credited to Thomas Jefferson, and Independence Day is celebrated on the Fourth of July—often outside with a summertime picnic. So here's a refreshing, wine-based summertime cocktail even Thomas could love.

The Strawberry Spritzer

5 oz. chilled white wine (Riesling or Pinot Blanc recommended)
4–5 fresh strawberries, room temperature
4–5 strawberries, frozen
Soda water

Muddle the fresh strawberries in the bottom of a Collins glass until pulpy. Fill glass halfway with wine, add frozen strawberries, and top with a splash of soda water.

supply inevitably ran low. As a testament to Jefferson's big orders, in 1801 (his first year as president) he would often purchase his Madeira wine by the "pipe"—each pipe holding more than one hundred gallons—at a cost of approximately $350.00. Moreover, he once ordered 240 bottles of Hungarian wine with a price tag of over five hundred dollars.

As proof that TJ was apt to err on the side of caution, he once estimated that he needed more than four hundred bottles of champagne per year to entertain at the Executive Mansion but robustly rounded up that calculation to five hundred bottles (why be caught short?). One can easily see how Jefferson's pursuit of purchases for his wine cellar could rapidly put a dent in the twenty-five-thousand-dollar salary that he drew as president.

Sometimes the wine ran out fast. When the Marquis de Lafayette visited in November 1824, he stayed at Monticello for eleven days. Jefferson had not seen Lafayette in thirty-five years, and they greeted each other in a tearful embrace. As one can imagine, there were several elaborate dinners and much wine-drinking—at Jefferson's expense. After the famous French patriot had departed, Jefferson's correspondence contained a plea to a Richmond wine merchant for some bottles ("...must pray you send me a box of Claret of about two dozen by the first wagon....") to tide him over, as his own cellar was nearly empty and an expected European shipment was yet to arrive.

An examination of Jefferson's wine cellar in his last years reflects the financial stress he must have been feeling. It was still well stocked, but with less of the expensive wines; the cellar even held some very mediocre domestic vintages.

But even before that, Jefferson—a few years after leaving the presidency—was well aware of his precarious financial situation. In 1813, he petitioned Congress to sell them his personal library of more than six thousand volumes. The idea was to replace the library burned down by the British when the invaders torched Washington during the War of 1812, and Congress was receptive. For Jefferson it meant a much-welcomed financial infusion of nearly $24,000. But the majority of that money went to pay some major debts, and certainly Jefferson could not have afforded to return to the high living standards he maintained during his presidential years.

THE JEFFERSON BOTTLES

Was it the great historical wine find? Or a fraud? In 2007, an article in the *New Yorker* magazine ("The Jefferson Bottles" by Patrick Radden Keefe) examined the sale of some very expensive wines said to have once been owned—or at least purchased with intent to ship—by Thomas Jefferson. In 2008, Random House published a book on the same subject—*The Billionaire's Vinegar: The Mystery of the World's Most Expensive Bottle of Wine* by Benjamin Wallace. The story revolves around a cache of dark green wine bottles, at least one lettered with the word "Lafitte," the date of "1787," and the initials "Th.J" (supposedly Jefferson's mark). The bottles were extracted from a bricked-up cellar wall in an old Parisian domicile. The presumption is that these bottles

> I find friendship to be like wine, raw when new, ripened with age....

were originally purchased by Jefferson but essentially remained undiscovered from about the time of the French Revolution until well into the twentieth century.

Were the wealthy, modern-day purchasers of the "Jefferson bottles" duped? Or are the "Th.J" initialed bottles the real deal? In the legal sense—at least at this writing—much of the controversy is still unsettled. In 1985, one bottle of the "Jefferson wine" (a Bordeaux) brought more than $150,000 at auction. The London auction house catalog described it as "inestimable" in value. But skeptics might claim that a more accurate description would be "too good to be true." After examining the bottles, a historian connected to Monticello said she was dubious that Jefferson ever owned them.

LAST CALL .... 🔔

If the cost of an auctioned "Jefferson bottle" etched with the "Lafitte" name is beyond your means, do not despair. "Jefferson Tavern Ale"—a hefty but affordable libation from Yards Brewery in Philadelphia—can deliver a good bang for the buck of the discerning beer drinker.

JAMES

MADISON

★ 1809–1817 ★

"IF MEN WERE ANGELS, NO GOVERNMENT
WOULD BE NECESSARY."

—James Madison

TOASTING [AT] THE EXECUTIVE MANSION

JAMES MADISON is often called "the Father of the Constitution" for drafting America's founding document. Madison also deserves partial credit for writing *The Federalist* papers with John Jay and Alexander Hamilton. Serving as Thomas Jefferson's secretary of state, Madison helped negotiate the Louisiana Purchase in 1803.

Madison became president in 1809, serving two terms. He presided over the War of 1812 (deemed "Mr. Madison's War" by his political foes) and endured the defeat of American troops at the Battle of Bladensburg, Maryland, as well as the humiliating burning of Washington (including the Executive Residence) that followed.

Like his good friend James Monroe, Madison was influenced by, and benefitted from, Jefferson's vast knowledge and appreciation of wine. In fact, Madison—like fellow Virginians Jefferson, Monroe, and John Tyler—championed wine (as opposed to whiskey) as a healthier and more respectable choice of alcohol for the American people.

Entertaining at the Executive Mansion or even at Montpelier (his plantation in Virginia), Madison was rarely naturally at ease. But while Madison may not have been the most gregarious host, his charming wife Dolley seems to have more than made up for it.

WINE VS. WHISKEY

James Madison Sr., the future president's father, had whiskey at the tobacco plantation—Montpelier—in the bucolic Virginia piedmont. But when it came to alcoholic preferences, Junior followed Thomas Jefferson, his presidential predecessor and fellow Virginian. That meant Madison saw wine as a positive addition to American culture and whiskey-swilling as a negative one—except when it could be used to swell the coffers of the U.S. Treasury, of course.

In 1817, Madison wrote to then president James Monroe, lauding his successor for "an overflowing Treasury" at a time when other countries were accumulating crippling debt. Madison then encouraged Monroe to keep up the tax on whiskey—despite its controversial status dating back to Washington's day.

> May it not, however, deserve consideration whether the still tax, which is a moralizing as well as a very easy, productive tax, would not be advantageously retained.... Why not press on the whisky drinkers rather than the tea and coffee drinkers, or the drinkers of the lighter kinds of wine?

Moreover, Madison was very receptive to the development of American wines—an idea about which Monroe and Jefferson also were quite keen, although native vineyards struggled to achieve even modest success in their era. Nevertheless, when the American viticulturist and winemaker John Adlum wrote to Madison stressing the virtues of grapes grown on native ground, he found an enthusiastic ally. After Adlum sent Madison a bottle of native-grown Tokay wine, the former president replied:

> It is so long since I tasted the celebrated wine whose name you have adopted, that my memory cannot compare its flavour with that of your specimen from an American grape. I am safe, I believe, in saying that the latter has an affinity to the general character

of the good Hungarian wines, and that it can scarcely
fail to recommend itself to discriminating palates.

In the same letter, Madison writes: "The introduction of a
native wine is not a little recommended." He notes that an American wine might serve the dual purpose of replacing expensive
vintages imported from Europe and encouraging Americans to
back off on more "ardent liquors" (i.e. whiskey and rum), which
he believed to be "destructive" to "the morals, the health, and the
social happiness of the American people."

THE HARVEST TIME HOP

It was common practice in Madison's day that large landowners
would dole out cups of whiskey to their workers during the strenuous harvest time. But given Madison's disdain for that powerful
liquor, it is not surprising that the retired president attempted to
substitute beer in place of the hard stuff. That action led to an amusing anecdote (recounted in Ralph Ketcham's *James Madison: A Biography*), as observed by the early American writer James K. Paulding,
when he and Madison were riding around the grounds at Montpelier.

> Mr. Madison had undertaken to substitute Beer in
> the room of whiskey, as a beverage for his slaves in
> Harvest time, and on one occasion, I remember stopt
> on a wheat field... to inquire how they liked the new
> drink—"O! ver fine masser" said one old grey head—
> "but I tink a glass of whiskey vere good to make it
> wholesome!" He [Madison] was excessively diverted
> at this supplement of the old fellow, and often made
> merry with it afterwards.

THE GREAT CHAMPAGNE EXPERIMENT

In her book *The First Forty Years of Washington Society*, Margaret Bayard
Smith provides some insightful scenes from the

WHISKEY FOR DOLLEY

The studious and often sickly James Madison was often over-shadowed by his gregarious wife, Dolley Madison. She does so again in the matter of cocktail drinking, as her husband merely preferred wine and she fancied a whiskey punch. But making punches can be a long and laborious task, so Dolley surely would have appreciated a quick and easy whiskey sour.

Dolley's Whiskey Sour

3 oz. bourbon whiskey (Virginia Gentleman would be appropriate)
1½ oz. lemon juice
1 oz. lime juice
4 tsp. powdered sugar

Combine all ingredients in a cocktail shaker and shake until the sugar is dissolved. Pour into two old fashioned glasses filled with ice.

> ...bottle after bottle came in.... Its only effects were animated good humour and uninterrupted conversation.

post-Revolutionary, pre–Civil War era. One such glimpse includes a letter from her husband, Samuel Harrison Smith, describing James Madison and an experiment with more than a few glasses of champagne. The champagne party took place in 1804 (during Thomas Jefferson's first term) when Madison was secretary of state:

> Have just returned, my dearest Margaret, from a dinning party at Genl. Dearborn's, where I met with Mrs. Madison and Mrs. Duval... I have rarely spent more agreeable hours at a dinner table. Mr. Granger, who was present and who is a very agreeable man, after a few bottles of champagne were emptied, on the observation of Mr. Madison that it was the most delightful wine when drank in moderation, but that more than a few glasses always produced a headache the next day, remarked with point that this was the very time to try the experiment, as the next day being Sunday would allow time for a recovery from its effects. The point was not lost upon the host and bottle after bottle came in, without however I assure you the least invasion of sobriety. Its only effects were animated good humour and uninterrupted conversation.

THE HOUSE WINE

Not all of Margaret Bayard Smith's historical memories were quite so lighthearted. In late August of 1814, she fled Washington when British troops routed the Americans in the Battle of

Bladensburg and occupied the Executive Residence. (It was not yet officially called the "White House" in Madison's time.) Dolley Madison barely escaped capture; in fact, her dinner (cooked by her French chef and prepared for forty guests at a long table) was still warm when the British sailors and marines stormed the capital.

One British author noted that the wine—bottles of it lying in coolers near the table—was "very good." As a taunting entertainment, British admiral George Cockburn (who was keen to start burning down the Executive Residence in retaliation for the torching of York, Ontario, by American troops earlier in the war) forced a young American bookseller to join the enemy at the presidential table. Afterward, the king's men put the residence to the torch and "the heavens redden'd with the blaze." As Smith wrote in her memoirs:

> The day before Cockburn paid this house a visit and forced a young gentleman of our acquaintance to go with him,—on entering the dining room they found the table spread for dinner, left precipitally by Mrs. M,—he insisted on young Weightman's sitting down and drinking Jemmy's health, which was the only epithet he used whenever he spoke of the President.

The president and Mrs. Madison enjoyed a well-stocked wine cellar at the Executive Residence—by some accounts, one thousand bottles. But apparently the bulk (though not all) of it escaped both the insult of satisfying British palates and the subsequent conflagration. It was a small consolation to the humbling defeat at the hands of the British Lion. "Mrs. M. lost all her own property," Smith noted. "The wine, of which there was a great quantity, was consumed by our own soldiers."

The reason most of the wine was consumed by retreating Americans was that the French staff member—one Jean Pierre Sioussat—set out buckets of wine and water, anticipating that thirsty troops would be in need of refreshment. And indeed they were:

American troops were hustling through Washington at great haste, the redcoats in spirited pursuit like hounds on an English foxhunt.

POP STAR

Years after the "Great Champagne Experiment," Madison, now president of the United States, remained wary of the imported French bubbly. In fact, Madison was aware that the celebratory wine could be explosive—both figuratively and literally.

Isaac Briggs, a noted surveyor of the post-Revolutionary era, visited President Madison a few days before Christmas 1816. (Briggs had performed years of surveying services for President Jefferson after the United States acquired the vast Louisiana

> Dolly [sic] attempted to open a bottle of Champagne wine, the cork flew to a distant corner of the room with an explosion as loud as— the sound of a popgun.

Purchase in 1803 and was on friendly terms with both Jefferson and Madison.) He found the president in a delightful mood and readily accepted when Madison invited him to return in the late afternoon for a "potluck" dinner. Briggs, who had been born a Quaker, was nonetheless amused by an incident that occurred after he "partook of an excellent family dinner." He included this anecdote in a letter to his wife:

> Dolly [sic] attempted to open a bottle of Champagne wine, the cork flew to a distant corner of the room with an explosion as loud as—the sound of a popgun. She looked scared, and the wine seemed to be in a haste to follow the cork. She however dexterously filled 3 large glasses, one for me, one for her sister

Lucy Washington [Todd], and one for herself. She handed the bottle to her husband but he would not take more than half-a-glass; I remarked after tasting it that it was very treacherous wine—yes, said the President addressing himself to Lucy, if you drink too much of it, it will make you hop like a cork. Dolly [sic] and Lucy, however, both took 2 glasses, but they soon afterwards left the table and retired—one glass and a half was as much as my head could bear without feeling uncomfortable.

LAST CALL..........................

While a student at the College of New Jersey (which became Princeton University in 1896), Madison, like many college students of that era, enjoyed "small" beer (light beer) and hard cider at the dinner table.

Madison lost one of his earliest elections for a Virginia delegate office when his opponent outspent him and supplied lavish amounts of whiskey to the voters.

JAMES

MONROE

★ 1817–1825 ★

"I HOPE WE SHALL RECEIVE [AN EXPECTED
SHIPMENT OF WINE], SINCE TO ME IT WILL BE A
MOST ACCEPTABLE ACCOMMODATION HAVING HAD
NONE OF ANY KIND FOR A LONG TIME."

—James Monroe

THE ERA OF
GOOD FEELING

NOBODY COULD EVER QUESTION the patriotism of James
Monroe, the man who became the fifth president of the
United States. The Virginian was not even nineteen
years old when he took a musket ball in his left shoulder as the
American army swarmed over the Hessians in the stormy
surprise attack at Trenton. Held in high esteem by General
George Washington (though their relationship later soured),
young Monroe also formed a lasting friendship with the Marquis de Lafayette during the struggle for independence.

When the Revolutionary War ended, Monroe was called
upon to serve diplomatic stints in Paris, where he helped
negotiate the Louisiana Purchase on behalf of President
Thomas Jefferson in 1803. While in Paris Monroe, like
Jefferson before him, acquired a taste for both French cuisine and French wines.

Andrew Jackson's great victory over the British at New
Orleans in 1815 got the attention and respect of European
powers. So when Monroe followed his friend James Madison to the presidency, he inherited one of the most tran-
quil periods of American history: the so-called "Era of
Good Feeling."

Along with his secretary of state, John Quincy Adams,
Monroe put forth a strong foreign policy, including the
renowned Monroe Doctrine. When not on the job, Monroe enjoyed the finer aspects of life, and that certainly
included wonderful wines with his lavish dinners.

THE TRIALS OF THE TOAST

In Monroe's era, diplomats, politicians, and, indeed, all who claimed to be gentlemen, were extremely sensitive to protocol and slights—real or perceived. Toasts and seating arrangements often brought these incidents of social tightrope-walking to the forefront. Blatant insults, of course, called for some sort of counteraction, such as demanding an apology. But in the crazy heyday of dueling, it was also common to issue a challenge to meet an offender on the "field of honor." (Monroe, in fact, came quite close to dueling Alexander Hamilton in 1792, prior to Hamilton's deadly duel with Aaron Burr in 1804.)

One such incident during Monroe's diplomatic career occurred when he was squeezed in between two minor German diplomats at a table in London. Monroe apparently felt testy about a seating arrangement that seemed, at best, an afterthought if not a deliberate slight, given that German mercenaries had nearly killed him at Trenton. So as toasts (sometimes called "sentiments" in that era) began, he placed his wine glass upside-down in the finger bowl when "The King!" was toasted.

Keep in mind that the Revolutionary War had ended merely twenty years earlier and the War of 1812 loomed just a few years in the future. Relations between England and its former colony remained as chilly as a Scottish loch.

Noticing Monroe's pique, the Russian ambassador stepped up and proposed a toast to the new president of the United States, and Monroe—his diplomatic feathers (and ego) now somewhat smoothed—rose to the occasion. Monroe then reciprocated with a toast to his new ally: "The health and prosperity of our friend, the Emperor of Russia!"

> Monroe then reciprocated with a toast to his new ally.

WHAT A PAINE

Thomas Paine—the fiery, hard-drinking author of *Common Sense*—lived in Paris after the American Revolution. But the English-born pamphleteer ran afoul of the leaders of the French Revolution (by, for example, openly objecting to capital punishment) and found himself imprisoned for ten months in 1794. His detractors claimed alcohol was at least partly responsible for his pigheadedness. As one noted: "He was a great drunkard [in Paris], and Mr. M., a merchant of this city, who lived with him when he was arrested by order of Robespierre, tells me he was intoxicated when that event happened."

Gouverneur Morris, one of the signers of the Declaration of Independence, was the American minister in Paris and Monroe's predecessor in that office. Morris—a Federalist senator from New York—disliked the radically inclined Paine, as he openly documented in his diary:

> [Paine] came to my house in company with Colonel Oswald, and, being a little more drunk than usual, behaved extremely ill, and through his insolence, I discovered his vain ambition. At present, I am told, he is besotted from morning till night.

So Morris did nothing to free Paine and, instead, concentrated on shipping his own precious wine collection back to the United States. That included some bottles of imperial Tokay that had once belonged to the guillotined queen, Marie Antoinette, as the sly and thrifty Morris had managed to snatch them up at a ridiculously low price. Successful in this venture, Morris embarked on some European travel, while Paine languished in prison.

When Monroe arrived in Paris, he immediately set to work to free Paine (as well as the wife of his former brother-in-arms, the Marquis de Lafayette) and finally managed to succeed with both of these delicate cases. When Paine was sprung, he was suffering from a terrible fever. Monroe's wife, Elizabeth, patiently nursed

CHATHAM ARTILLERY PUNCH

It was allegedly labeled "suave and deceitful" by President Monroe when he supposedly sampled some on his 1819 visit to the port city of Savannah, Georgia. The recipe typically features an array of alcohol. Obviously this recipe is intended for dozens and dozens of experienced imbibers:

Chatham Artillery Punch

1½ gal. strong tea	½ pt. Benedictine
1½ gal. Catawba or scuppernong wine	2½ lbs. brown sugar
½ gal. rum	1 bottle of maraschino cherries
1½ qt. rye whiskey	juice of 18 oranges
1 qt. brandy	juice of 18 lemons
1 qt. gin	1 case of champagne

Prep: First pour all the ingredients, except for the champagne, into a non-reactive container. Second: Let it rest for a day and a half to two days. Third: Just before the celebration, dump into an extra-large punch bowl or tub over lots of ice, and then add the champagne. Four: Make sleeping arrangements for any over-indulgers, or bring in a battalion of designated drivers.

Paine back to health. Given the medical practices of the times, alcohol almost certainly would have been part of that process.

Paine—drunk, sober, or feverish—plotted revenge against George Washington because he felt that the president (like Morris) had done nothing to help him in his hour of need. But he moved out of Monroe's house before he began to abuse Washington, at least with any real venom. He no doubt realized his benefactor was in a delicate situation—representing the president but harboring one of Washington's most vocal (and rare) critics. As for Monroe, he sensed what was coming and wrote to his friend James Madison on July 5, 1796, expressing that exact worry: "[Paine] thinks the President winked at his imprisonment and wished he might die in gaol, and bears him resentment for it; also he is preparing an attack upon him of the most virulent kind."

And Paine soon launched this attack. In his famous open letter to George Washington, for example, Paine stormed: "The world will be puzzled to decide whether you are an apostate or an imposter; whether you have abandoned good principles or whether you ever had any."

Paine died in Greenwich Village, New York, in 1809. By some accounts he was drinking several bottles of rum a week just prior to his death—but, given the era, it might have been viewed as an acceptable medical strategy to combat his illnesses.

WHERE'S OUR WINE?

> Ever the Virginia country squire, Monroe usually chose wine.

Unlike his compatriot Paine, Monroe was not a consistent imbiber of rum. Ever the Virginia country squire, Monroe usually chose wine. Like his friend James Madison, Monroe was greatly influenced by Thomas Jefferson in regards to wine. Although the Virginians dabbled in attempts to grow their own vineyards (with very

SYLLABUB

On the other end of the alcohol recipe spectrum, consider Monroe's "Syllabub" dessert. It requires far less alcohol, far less prep time, and will dispense with the need for extra sleeping bags.

The origins of this dessert trace back to Old England, but the colonials—and then the new Americans—did not hold that fact against it. Syllabub was a light, refreshing dessert that would have been perfect for hot, sultry summer evenings in Virginia.

Syllabub

1½ c. of whipping cream
juice of 2 lemons
½ c. sugar
½ c. white wine
¼ c. dry sherry

Whisk the whipping cream until it gets slightly thick. Add the lemon juice, sugar, white wine, and sherry to the cream—one at a time—whisking after each new addition. Whisk this batch until it gets thick, three to five minutes. Pour promptly into parfait glasses and refrigerate overnight. The concoction will separate when it stands. You can top it off with more whipped cream prior to serving.

little success), they depended primarily on imports for their best bottles.

And so we find James Monroe contacting Madison (and we can almost sense his frustration) about a wine shipment that both men had apparently been anxiously awaiting. On July 13, 1799, Monroe (soon to be governor of Virginia) felt compelled to write Madison:

> Dear Sir
>   Have you ever rec. y. wine from Mr. Yard? I hope we shall receive it, since to me, it will be a most acceptable accommodation having had none of any kind for a long time; and if it really is of the quality we are taught to expect of it, it will also be of importance to you.

And then, as if to emphasize the urgency, Monroe pleads: "If you have not written for it, had you not better yet do it?"

THE "LIQUID FURNITURE" FUND

After becoming president in 1817, Monroe embarked on a mission to bring the Executive Mansion decor up to his exacting standards. To suit his Francophile tastes, Monroe imported luxury furniture from France and had other pieces made by skilled craftsmen. Congress had provided twenty thousand dollars for these endeavors, but Monroe soon exceeded that amount and brought in some of his own personal furnishings to bolster the redecorating efforts.

Unfortunately for Monroe, he put Colonel Samuel Lane in charge of the payments of the furniture fund, and Lane seemingly made a mess of it. But the full extent of that mess was not discovered until after Lane's death in 1822.

One of Lane's questionable maneuvers was the acquisition of 1,200 bottles of Burgundy wine and champagne from France that—carelessly or purposely—got charged to the furniture account.

That, and similar errors, resulted in Monroe's unpleasant surprise of finding he owed various creditors several thousands of dollars.

All but Monroe's most ardent enemies believed him to be personally innocent of these miscalculations concerning the wine. As Thomas Jefferson once reportedly said of him: "Monroe was so honest that if you turned his soul inside out there would not be a spot on it."

THE PLANTATION TOUCH

Monroe, like many of the pre–Civil War presidents, owned slaves and brought some servants to the Executive Mansion. The house slaves served dinners and drinks at parties—often called "levees" in Monroe's time. As a Mrs. Tuley of Virginia described a New Year's reception at the Executive Mansion:

> All the lower rooms were open and though well filled, not uncomfortable. The rooms were warmed by great fires of hickory wood in the large open fireplaces, and with the handsome brass and irons and fenders quite remind me of our grand old wood fires in Virginia. Wine was handed about in wine glasses on large silver salvers, by colored waiters dressed in dark livery, gilt buttons, etc. I suppose some of them must have come from Mr. Monroe's old family seat, Oak Hill, Virginia.

LAST CALL

As a young officer in the Revolution, Monroe (as did most soldiers) drank whenever the army had—or captured—stores of liquor. Monroe's immediate superior during the war was Lord Stirling (William Alexander), and allegedly one of Monroe's camp duties was to keep his commander's glass full.

When the Marquis de Lafayette made his U.S. tour in 1824–1825 (about fifty years after the Revolution began), he stopped to see his old friend Monroe (first at the Executive Mansion and then later at Oak Hill), and many toasts were offered in the celebrated Frenchman's honor.

JOHN QUINCY

ADAMS

★ 1825–1829 ★

"WE GOT TO SINGING AFTER SUPPER, AND THE BOTTLE
WENT ROUND WITH AN UNUSUAL RAPIDITY, UNTILL, A
ROUND DOZEN HAD DISAPPEARED. I THEN THOUGHT IT
WAS HIGH TIME TO RETREAT...."

—John Quincy Adams

A DIARIST
AND DRINKER

THE FIRST SON of a president to become president, John Quincy Adams was the stereotypical New Englander—flinty, blunt, and slow-to-warm. But at least he was self-aware. The country's sixth president confessed that he lacked "the honey" to ever be a "true flycatcher."

Like his father, John Quincy Adams was a dedicated diarist, but he certainly did not have the capacity (or urge) for drinking that his father did. Perhaps he was nudged toward moderation by a rare head-butt with the power of alcohol when he was a law student. It was a lopsided confrontation: Adams was left with a lingering, three-day hangover and a wary respect for his liquid adversary.

But Adams more than held his own against powerful political opponents of his era, chief among them the volatile Andrew Jackson, known as "Old Hickory." A Federalist, Adams also sometimes clashed with Henry Clay but was not above alliances with Clay.

Adams was a sore loser. When Jackson—his arch nemesis—swept him from office after just one term, JQA bolted for New England before Inauguration Day dawned in Washington. But he eventually returned to the capital as a U.S. Congressman in 1831. John Quincy Adams died on February 21, 1848, after collapsing in the House chamber. One of his honorary pallbearers was a wet-behind-the-ears congressman from Illinois by the name of Abraham Lincoln.

HARVARD DAYS

Just prior to entering Harvard in 1786, a teenage John Quincy Adams proclaimed in a December 31, 1785, diary entry: "Whatever errors, or foibles, may have mislead me... at least I have not to reproach myself with Vice, which has always been my principle to dread, and my Endeavor to shun."

JQA probably did not pursue "Vice" (even with a small "v") with any real vigor during his year at Harvard (given junior status upon entry, he graduated in 1786). But as a member of Phi Beta Kappa, he did sometimes cut loose at their celebrations, as noted at one such gathering: "Wit and wine, the Bottle and the Joke, kept nearly an equal pace. When the Prayer Bell rung we broke up, and attended Prayers."

But in the same year, Adams voiced his disapproval of a celebration that took place on the site of one of the Revolution's early battles (one that Adams, as a young boy, had witnessed from afar). In his entry of June 17, he recorded: "A Dinner was provided for 600 People on Bunker's hill: the havoc of oxen, sheep, and fowls of all kinds... and I dare say, there was as much wine drank now, as there was blood spilt then."

> ...I dare say, there was as much wine drank now, as there was blood spilt then.

As for fellow students that did overindulge, Adams does mention some of the more outrageous incidents, and one can almost sense his disdain. Of one student who broke his leg, Adams reported that he was "drunk as a beast." And he detailed the untimely tumble of another in his diary (November 24, 1786):

> This evening, just after tea... we were called out by the falling of a fellow, from the top of the stairs. He was in liquor and fell in such a manner, that his head was on the lower floor, and his feet two or three steps up... the blood was streaming from his head, his eyes

appeared fixed, and he was wholly motionless. We all supposed him dead. He soon recovered, however....

JQA'S FANTASTIC FROLIC

In John Quincy Adams's day, going on a "frolick" usually equated to "a bender" or "a binge" in modern terminology. Although Adams seems to have been quite temperate during his college days, he definitely (though rarely) overindulged as a law student.

In fact, JQA was blindsided by a liquid learning experience in late September 1787. It started innocently enough with Adams stopping by to enjoy dinner with friends. But whatever they washed down their supper with (madeira? rum?) soon got the upper hand. As his entry of September 29 records:

> In the evening I took something of a long walk with Townsend; and as I return'd stopp'd to sup; upon the birds, which Amory and Stacey, had been hunting for in the course of the day. There were three other gentlemen there, Mr. Coffin, Mr. Winslow, and a Captain Cochran. We got to singing after supper, and the bottle went round with an unusual rapidity, untill, a round dozen had disappeared. I then thought it was high time to retreat, and with some difficulty slip'd away from those of the company, who appeared to be the most inspired....

But Adams's "retreat" apparently did not come soon enough, as the next day's entry (despite an initial reluctance to admit that he had overindulged) soon makes clear:

> Although I had not last night, been guilty of an excess so far as to be intoxicated, yet I had not sufficiently consulted what my feelings would be this day, to be entirely prudent. I therefore arose this morning, with

THE RUSSIANS ARE COMING

Before he became president, John Quincy Adams was appointed by President James Madison to be the first ever U.S. Minister to Russia, where he spent nearly five years in an official capacity and attended many social engagements in St. Petersburg. While the cocktail known as the White Russian was not invented for more than a century after Adams's death, it seems an appropriate beverage to honor our sixth president.

White Russian
2 oz. vodka
1 oz. Kahlua or other coffee liqueur
1 oz. light cream

Add all ingredients into a cocktail shaker half-filled with ice cubes. Shake well and strain into an old fashioned glass filled with ice.

a very disagreeable headache, which continued the whole day. I could neither attend meeting nor read, nor write; and pass'd the day with much tediousness.

There is a tone of incredulousness to JQA's next entry of October 1, a Monday. He is somewhat stunned that he is still suffering; his claims of not actually having been intoxicated have disappeared, and are replaced by some regrets.

I have not yet got over the consequences of our frolick on Saturday evening. Three whole evenings I have by this means entirely lost, for I cannot yet write with any comfort. How inseparably in all cases of intemperance, is the punishment allied to the fault!

ONCE BITTEN, TWICE SHY

Less than a month later, Adams indulged at a friend's engagement celebration—but he was among the cautious few.

At Twelve we went to Mr. Thaxter's lodgings, and found fifty or sixty people heartily at work, in which we readily joined them. At about 2, there were 18 to 20 left who sat down to a table covered with "big bellied bottles." For 2 hours or more Bacchus and Momus joined hands to increase the festivity of the Company. But the former of these deities then of a sudden took a fancy to divert himself, and fell to tripping up their heels... by five o'clock they were all under the table except those who had been peculiarly cautious....

Among the "peculiarly cautious" must have been JQA, because the next day's diary entry proudly recorded: "Rose at about 8 this morning, and felt no inconveniency from the scene of yesterday...."

CLASHING WITH CLAY

Adams knew full well that Henry Clay—so avid an enthusiast of gambling and whiskey that his governmental duties sometimes seemed like an afterthought—wielded considerable political clout. On more than one occasion in his career, JQA found himself forced to work with the famous Kentuckian. In fact, Andrew Jackson and his loyalists insisted that Adams and Clay had colluded—the infamous "corrupt bargain"—to steal the election of 1824 from the "Hero of New Orleans." (It wasn't all that farfetched a conclusion; Clay had steered his votes to Adams and, after JQA was elected, Adams named Clay as his secretary of state.)

Adams, however, was quite clear about what he thought of Clay's questionable lifestyle, once snidely quipping that the senator's coat of arms should feature "a pistol, a pack of playing cards, and a bottle." Long before Adams ran for president, he glimpsed Clay's reveling lifestyle at close quarters when both men were in Ghent, Belgium, to hash out the complicated peace treaty with England following the War of 1812. In July of 1814, Adams's diary reflected his disgust toward Clay and some of the other American negotiators:

> I dined again at the table-d'hote at one. The other gentlemen dined together, at four. They sit after dinner and drink bad wine and smoke cigars, which suits neither my habits nor my health, and absorbs time which I cannot spare.

And later in the same year, Adams—stirring just before dawn as was his routine—wrote: "I heard Mr. Clay's company retiring from his chambers. I left him with Mr. Russell, Mr. Bentzon, and Mr. Todd at cards. They parted as I was about to rise."

THE TAZEWELL TOKAY TWEAK

As a man committed to the Andrew Jackson camp, Littleton Waller Tazewell—a Virginian elected to the U.S. Senate in 1824—

was a natural foe in the eyes of John Quincy Adams. Consequently, JQA simply couldn't resist tweaking Tazewell when the opportunity arose. And that opportunity arose not over some crucial piece of legislation, but over wine.

At a well-attended Executive Mansion dinner, Tazewell proclaimed that Rhenish wine and Tokay wine tasted alike. Adams, who had definitely sipped Tokay wine while in Europe, all but sniffed in contempt: "Sir... I do not believe you ever drank a drop of Tokay in your life."

Had someone dropped a fork on the floor, certainly the rattle and clank would have reverberated through the Executive Mansion. Adams issued what must have been a halfhearted apology (days later and through an intermediary), and Tazewell accepted it "officially" (but doubtless unwillingly). Adams didn't believe Tazewell's acceptance was genuine, noting in his diary: "...the shaft was sped barbed with truth, and it will rankle in [Tazewell's] side till his dying hour."

LAST CALL

Like his father, JQA knew his Madeira well. He often drank two or three glasses of the strong wine in a sitting. Famously, JQA reportedly once "taste-tested" fourteen kinds of Madeira—and successfully identified eleven of them. As one of his biographers concluded, a drinker of the amateur ranks could not have accomplished such a feat.

ANDREW

JACKSON

★ 1829–1837 ★

"I HAVE NEVER IN MY LIFE SEEN A KENTUCKIAN
WHO DIDN'T HAVE A GUN, A PACK OF CARDS, AND
A JUG OF WHISKEY."

—Andrew Jackson

OLD HICKORY

WHEN THE BRITISH ATTEMPTED to invade New Orleans shortly before Christmas in 1814, Andrew Jackson supposedly bellowed: "I will smash them, so help me God!" And he did exactly that, soundly repulsing the British at the Battle of New Orleans on January 8, 1815, earning the nickname of "Old Hickory" (as in, "tough as old hickory"). His battlefield heroics eventually helped him become the seventh president of the United States.

Jackson's election dismayed his political rivals, including Henry Clay of Kentucky, who snidely said: "I cannot believe that the killing of 2500 Englishmen at New Orleans qualifies a person for the various, difficult, and complicated duties of the Chief Magistracy."

Despite being a slave-owner, President Jackson was a strong Unionist and famously faced down John C. Calhoun and South Carolina on the issue of Nullification (the notion that a state has the right to nullify, or invalidate, any federal law that that state has deemed unconstitutional).

Like more than a few general-presidents, Jackson was more skillful on the battlefield than he was in addressing complex economic or banking issues. Some historians believe that the ineptness of Jackson's policies helped create the Panic of 1837, a severe downturn that featured numerous bank failures and a depression that lasted for several years.

WHISKEY FOR PISTOLS

Like George Washington, Andrew Jackson enjoyed the profits from a whiskey-making still—both at his historic homestead, the Hermitage, and also prior to that at his lesser-known Hunter's Hill Farm. Jackson's letters and account books include more than a few references to whiskey, and it is obvious that he often used the powerful liquor made of rye and corn in place of hard money to pay for various items and debts. He also sold it at some small stores that he owned in the Nashville area. In September 1799, the man who would become famous for defending New Orleans against the British invasion wrote this letter to Robert Hays.

> Dear Sir—This morning your Pistols was handed to me by Mr. Brawley together with your letter for which I thank you. The whiskey you can have at any time in such quantities as you may think proper, or as you may require....

That the brace of pistols were greatly valued by Jackson should not be a surprise; he fought in several serious duels, brawls, and donnybrooks in his lifetime.

TRASHING THE EXECUTIVE MANSION

Jackson supporters would say their hero was—first and foremost—a "man of the people." But Jackson's detractors were equally insistent that Old Hickory's most loyal followers were "rabble."

In the wild aftermath of Jackson's first inauguration in 1829, it was difficult to argue with the latter assessment. After the new president was sworn in, thousands (crowd estimates ranged from ten thousand to thirty thousand) swarmed after Jackson's carriage as he made his way to the President's House. Supreme Court associate justice Joseph Story remarked that the overflow included the "highest and most polished... down to the most vulgar and gross in the nation." He further exclaimed, "I never saw such a mixture. The reign of King Mob seemed triumphant. I was glad to escape from the scene as soon as possible."

> Thousands of Jackson's followers ... were offered—at the Executive Mansion, no less—buckets of spiked orange punch and wine to continue the celebration.

The situation became increasingly precarious once the president was in the Executive Mansion. Rough men, their boots caked with street slop, stood on once-dainty chairs to get a view of the Hero of New Orleans. The unwashed and uneducated pressed forward to offer Jackson their congratulations. Had his back not already been against the wall, surely they would have slapped him hard between the shoulder blades. At one point, Jackson's men needed to form a protective barrier around the president to prevent him from being crushed by the surging masses.

Liquor played a role in this chaotic scenario. Thousands of Jackson's followers had been drinking toasts at his inauguration earlier in the day, and then they were offered—at the Executive Mansion, no less—buckets of spiked orange punch and wine to continue the celebration.

In the end, the rowdy crowd was coaxed outside only after the buckets of punch and wine were dispersed around the Executive Mansion grounds. Old Hickory's supporters climbed out windows to get to the liquor to soothe their throats, most raspy from the repetitive shouts of "Huzzah!" during the hours of jubilation. In the words of Margaret Bayard Smith, a Washington socialite of the era:

> But what a scene did we witness! The Majesty of the People had disappeared, and a rabble, a mob, of boys, negros [sic], women, children, scrambling, fighting, romping. What a pity! What a pity! No arrangements had been made no police officers placed on duty and the whole house had been inundated.

TOASTING OLD HICKORY'S VICTORY

Andrew Jackson made his name through his military leadership at the Battle of New Orleans during the War of 1812—literally. He was stern yet popular with his troops, who called him "tough as old hickory" on the battlefield. He has been referred to as Old Hickory ever since. In honor of Jackson's victory in New Orleans over the British, here is the official cocktail of New Orleans: the Sazerac.

The Sazerac
¼ oz. absinthe (or Pernod)
1 sugar cube
2 dashes Peychaud bitters
2 oz. rye whiskey
1 lemon twist

Take a chilled old-fashioned glass and coat it with the absinthe. Add crushed ice and set the glass aside. In a mixing glass, place sugar cube and add bitters to it, then crush the sugar cube. Pour in the whiskey, add ice, and stir. Empty the chilled glass of the crushed ice and strain the whiskey concoction into it. Add the lemon twist for garnish.

The President, after having been literally nearly pressed to death and almost suffocated and torn to pieces by the people in their eagerness to shake hands with Old Hickory, had retreated through the back way or south front and had escaped to his lodgings at Gadsby's [tavern].

Cut glass and china to the amount of several thousand dollars had been broken in the struggle to get to the refreshments, punch and other articles had been carried out in tubs and buckets, but had it been in hogsheads it would have been insufficient... for 20,000 people, for it is said that number was there, tho' I think the number exaggerated.

WILD YOUTH

Andrew Jackson was sixty-one years old by the time he reached the Executive Mansion. His hard drinking days were long behind him. He was, in fact, in serious grief over the recent death of his beloved wife Rachel. Even his infamous temper was less easily triggered. The duels he had fought, including one that left bullets embedded in his body, had also taken a physical toll on his health. He was less than robust—except in the political arena, where he was still a formidable force.

Young Andy Jackson grew up hardscrabble poor in North Carolina and suffered punishment from the redcoats during the Revolution, but his earliest biographers found ample evidence that he had raised his fair share of hell and hijinks. Jackson biographer James Parton quoted a Salisbury, North Carolina, resident who remembered the young man of Scotch-Irish stock in this way: "Andrew Jackson was the most roaring, rollicking, game-cocking, horse-racing, card-playing, mischievous fellow that ever lived in Salisbury."

Parton (who talked to Salisbury residents for a book on Jackson published just prior to the Civil War) also landed the following gem from a woman who recalled her incredulous reaction when she'd heard Jackson was a candidate for the highest office in the land: "What! Jackson up for President? Jackson? Andrew Jackson? The Jackson that used to live in Salisbury? Why, when he was here, he was such a rake that my husband would not bring him into the house!" (Then she paused and eased up slightly.) "It is true, he might have taken him out to the stable to weigh horses for a race, and might drink a glass of whiskey with him there. Well, if Andrew Jackson can be President, anybody can!"

> Well, if Andrew Jackson can be President, anybody can!

Even after Jackson began to ascend the ladder of success (he was already a lawyer at age twenty-one and a congressman by twenty-nine), he never gave up his love of horseracing, cockfighting, billiards, and cards. His biographer Parton—with something of a "wink" to his readers—wrote of Jackson's early adulthood:

> Betting in all its varieties was carried on continually…. The whisky bottle—could that be wanting?
>
> In all these sports—the innocent and the less innocent—Andrew Jackson was an occasional participant. He played billiards and cards, and both for money. He ran horses and bet on the horses of others. He was occasionally hilarious over his whisky or his wine, when he came to Nashville on Saturdays. At the cockpit no man more eager than he. There are gentlemen of the first respectability now living at Nashville who remember seeing him often at the cock-pit in the public square adjoining the old Nashville inn, cheering on his favorite birds with loudest vociferation.

WINE TO THE WOUNDED

Like many gentlemen of his era, Andrew Jackson had a keen "sense of honor"—which is to say, he did not take an insult, real or perceived, lightly. Jackson also had a quick temper. The combination led to several duels and brawls. In 1806, Jackson found himself *mano a mano* with a deadly skilled marksman—Charles Dickinson—in a pistol duel at a mere eight paces (about twenty-four feet) apart. Not surprisingly, some debts owed to Jackson from a horserace helped spark the argument, further fueled by an alleged insult to Jackson's wife, Rachel.

Wagers around Nashville had Dickinson as the pre-duel favorite. But Jackson—who dressed in a loose frock coat over his tall-but-wiry frame—failed to fall when his enemy's projectile caught him in the ribs, about a half-inch from his heart. Dickinson became wide-eyed with the assumption (a wrong one, as it turned out) that he had missed Jackson completely. But Jackson lined up his stunned adversary and coolly aimed his dueling pistol. Then, in the words of James Parton:

> The pistol neither snapped nor went off. He looked at the trigger, and discovered that it had stopped at half cock. He drew it back to its place and took aim a second time. He fired. Dickinson's face blanched; he reeled; his friends rushed toward him, caught him in their arms, and gently seated him on the ground.... The blood was rushing from his side in a torrent....

Jackson walked to a nearby house to get his own wound treated. But in the aftermath, he sent a bottle of wine to Dickinson's doctor to be used in the treatment of the man who had just tried to kill him on the so-called "field of honor." The gesture may have been gallant, but—wine or no wine—the doomed Dickinson did not survive.

THE BUMPKIN'S BEST

Before Jackson ascended to the presidency, his detractors assumed that he was an ill-tempered and inarticulate woodsman from a state barely above frontier status (Tennessee). The post-inauguration party—and the consequent damage inflicted on the Executive Mansion—only enhanced those impressions and prejudices.

But Jackson's entertaining at the Executive Mansion soon proved to be a wonderful surprise for even non-supporters who visited. Some of the credit had to go to Jackson's niece, Emily Donelson, who helped Executive Mansion events run smoothly. The dinners were lavish and the libations equally impressive.

Jackson would sometimes bring out whiskey for Executive Mansion visitors, occasionally sipping a glass himself. His wine cellar at the Executive Mansion was superb, and like most of the presidents before him, it included the best French wines (red and white), champagne, port, and Madeira.

JACKSON'S MOST FAMOUS TOAST

When Jackson was president, John C. Calhoun (his vice president at that time) was pushing the "states' rights" agenda. At the Thomas Jefferson Day dinner on April 13, 1830—a major affair for the Democrats—the ever-flinty Jackson showed up and proposed a toast: "Our Union!" he emphatically stated, lifting his glass. "It must be preserved!" Then Jackson, his point made, sat down.

This was not what the Nullification wing, mostly Southerners, wanted to hear. Calhoun, the South Carolinian, attempted to counter-toast with: "The Union—next to our liberty the most dear. May we all remember that it can only be preserved by respecting the rights of the States...." Some accounts claim that Calhoun's hand shook when he made his toast, spilling some wine.

THE HAIR-TRIGGER TEMPER

Although Jackson was quite familiar with alcohol consumption, he didn't see drinking as an excuse to tarnish someone's honor—

specifically his own—without expecting some consequences. Samuel Southard, New Jersey senator and the secretary of the navy under John Quincy Adams (himself an anti-Jackson man), made the mistake of bad-mouthing Old Hickory at an 1826 dinner gathering at which wine was consumed. Essentially, the senator suggested that Jackson's heroics at New Orleans in January 1815 had been exaggerated, and that James Monroe (then secretary of war) deserved the lion's share of the credit for ordering an army into the field to defeat the British in the first place.

Other than insulting his wife, nothing brought Jackson's Scotch-Irish temper to boil faster than the insinuation that his military record had anything less than a spit-polish shine to it. When word of Southard's remarks got back to him, an infuriated Jackson quickly dashed off a letter to his offender, outlining the facts (as Jackson saw them) concerning his defense of New Orleans.

Jackson—with his demonstrated willingness to participate in duels of honor—always had to be regarded as a loose cannon. The Princeton-educated Southard, well aware of this, soon sent back a letter with an "I-can't-recall-exactly-what-was-said" tone to it.

Jackson's return letter admonished Southard (and restated his own accomplishments at New Orleans). The general added:

> I have therefore to request when on your election-
> eering tours, or at your wine drinkings hereafter,
> you will not fail to recollect these historical facts,
> which indeed you ought long since have known....

Jackson eventually let the controversy fade away and Southard (who became governor of New Jersey) thereby managed to avoid the full force of the future president's infamous wrath. Southard, in fact, might thus have dodged a bullet—literally.

LAST CALL

When Jackson's beloved Hermitage caught fire in 1834, Old Hickory was quick to lament: "I suppose all the wines in the cellar have been destroyed?"

In the 1950s, Old Crow launched a series of advertisements promoting its bourbon. The ads depicted famous political figures from the nineteenth century, and Andrew Jackson was featured prominently in some of them.

MARTIN

VAN BUREN

★ 1837–1841 ★

"I STOPPED AT NEW YORK ONLY LONG ENOUGH TO
PAY THE BETS I HAD LOST ON THE STATE ELECTION..."

—Martin Van Buren

BLUE WHISKEY VAN

MARTIN VAN BUREN, the eighth president of the United States, notched more nicknames than any other commander in chief. Some of them were nods to his political aplomb, such as "The Little Magician" (which also noted his short stature), "The American Talleyrand" (after the crafty French diplomat), and "The Red Fox of Kinderhook" (which referenced his hair color and his birthplace in New York State).

For the purposes of this book, however, one must mention "Blue Whiskey Van"—a moniker that he acquired while campaigning in Hudson Valley taverns early in his political career. Something of a backhanded compliment, "Blue Whiskey Van" supposedly spoke to Van Buren's ability to drink significant amounts of alcohol without all the stumbling and mumbling that sometimes plague those less gifted in alcoholic tolerance. Apparently the eighth president of the United States could hold his liquor very well indeed—a talent that served him well, since electioneering in his day was accompanied by plenty of drinking.

Unfortunately, Van Buren was much less steady in addressing the Panic of 1837, which featured bank failures and massive unemployment—all of which undermined his presidency and helped sink his bid for a second term.

THE KINDERHOOK KID

Politics is full of ironies, and a prime example is certainly Van Buren's 1840 loss to William Henry Harrison's "Hard Cider" campaign.

The political operatives behind Harrison's Whig platform went to great lengths to convince the public that "Old Tip" was a man of humble nature (a log cabin dweller, no less!), while Van Buren (according to the Whigs) was an arrogant aristocrat who resided in a palace, supping on gourmet dinners chased down with expensive wines. While there was some truth to that depiction, Van Buren, by far, emerged from humbler beginnings than Harrison, who was born into a well-to-do Virginia plantation dynasty before moving west to Ohio and Indiana. In fact, Van Buren—the Jacksonian Democrat—had been born in a tavern in the small village of Kinderhook, New York, in 1782.

Abraham Van Buren, the future president's father, fought at the pivotal Battle of Saratoga in the Revolutionary War. He also owned an establishment that served as a watering hole, a spot to sell off the "liberated" belongings of hapless loyalists and, at times, a place to pick up one's mail. Young Martin (whose first language was Dutch) probably had a front-row seat for observing human nature and the intricacies of spirited debate (in Dutch, English, or an evolving hybrid of both) among the masses. It must have seemed logical to proceed to a career in law, followed by politics.

Harrison, by contrast, chose the army route. He took a page from the Andrew Jackson strategic outline: get famous for winning a few battles, then use that fame as a springboard to a political career. Harrison supposedly was content to drink hard cider, but that snooty, affluent Van Buren needed champagne and Madeira, among other European luxuries (such as fancy clothes and a coach), on a daily basis—at least, that was the Whig line.

Call it a flimflam, but the result was that Harrison (and running mate John Tyler) steamrolled the incumbent Van Buren in the 1840 presidential election. In fact, one political cartoon depicted just that—"Little Van" running for his life, with a rolling barrel of hard cider about to flatten him. It was an exaggeration only in the literal sense.

STEPPING UP FOR OLD HICKORY

An ardent Jackson Democrat, Van Buren was on hand on April 13, 1830, when Jackson, nicknamed Old Hickory, made his famous "Jefferson birthday dinner" speech against the anti-tariff Nullifiers—led by Jackson's own vice president, John C. Calhoun of South Carolina.

Jackson proposed a toast to his audience: "Our Union! It must be preserved!" The "Nullies" in the crowd reluctantly rose and sheepishly pretended to sip their wine in solemn acknowledgement of the president's words—strong and unmistakable in their message.

> He liked top-shelf liquor and lots of it.

At a mere five feet six inches, Van Buren was in danger of missing the historical moment, as taller and broader men rose before him in tense excitement. Van Buren later admitted: "When the President was called upon for his toast I was obliged to stand on my chair to get a distinct view of what passed in his vicinity."

Calhoun attempted to mitigate the damages from Jackson's words with his own toast, and Van Buren—then Jackson's secretary of state but destined to replace Calhoun as Old Hickory's vice president—followed with a toast that called for "mutual forbearance and reciprocal concessions...."

VAN THE [TOP-SHELF] MAN

The rumors about Van Buren liking the finer stuff in life, particularly when it came to libations or food, were not without foundation. He liked top-shelf liquor and lots of it.

A DUTCHMAN'S DRINK

Van Buren holds the distinction of being the only U.S. President for which English was his second language. He grew up speaking Dutch, as his birthplace of Kinderhook, New York, was isolated and largely populated by townspeople of Dutch descent. For "the Little Magician"—one of his many nicknames, this one a nod to his stature and political acumen—here is a cocktail appropriately dubbed "The Flying Dutchman."

The Flying Dutchman

2 oz. gin

½ oz. triple sec

Pour the ingredients into a mixing glass filled halfway with ice. Stir well and strain into an old-fashioned glass filled with ice.

By many reports, Van Buren handled his alcohol with commendable expertise. Since he was such a small man, "The Little Magician's" trickery in avoiding at least the outward appearance of alcohol's worst effects seems all the more remarkable. Van Buren biographer Holmes Alexander wrote in 1935:

> It was during this canvas of 1807 that [Van Buren] seems to have developed another reputation for which he was extraordinarily pleased—and to all reports, justly so. The reference here is to his capacity for imbibing enormous amounts of intoxicants without the usual result, and for which he earned the proud title of Blue Whiskey Van... this stood him in good stead, for most of the electioneering was done in the taprooms.

What did Van Buren drink? Many types of alcohol—although, despite the Blue Whiskey Van nickname, little of that hard liquor, especially in his later years. Van Buren's favorite libations started with the lighter table wines (including champagne), but he also enjoyed the heavier (and more alcoholic) Madeira, sherry, and after-dinner brandy. He sometimes splurged on the dark red Montepulciano wine from Italy (as did Thomas Jefferson before him).

Like Richard Nixon decades later, Van Buren was not above serving lesser-quality alcohol to his visitors. In November of 1831, Van Buren wrote William Rives, the former U.S. ambassador to France, requesting his help in snagging some top-notch vintages, but also some cheaper bottles "which will be good enough to give to my friends... a few degrees above what is usually used with water."

THE SCHIEDAM CONNECTION

One drink that the young Martin Van Buren must have sampled (and later offered to guests) was somewhat unique to the Dutch settlers of New York—Schiedam, a powerful clear alcohol. Schiedam got its name from a Dutch city renowned for manufacturing the stuff as early as the sixteenth century. By the seventeenth century, distilleries in Schiedam were shipping their potent product to London, where apparently it hit the lower classes with a head-spinning smack. (England, in turn, shipped much of its grain to Holland, which the Dutch turned into more alcohol.)

The Dutch called this drink Jenever—and its English consumers knew it as "Dutch gin," or "Schiedam," in deference to the city that made so much of it. (As if to further testify to its wallop, one who downed a few ounces of Dutch gin—followed by a glass of lager beer as "a chaser"—is sometimes said to have experienced a *kopstoot*, a "head-butt" in Dutch.)

Describing one of Van Buren's earliest campaigns (in 1808), historian Holmes Alexander put Schiedam front and center:

> The system of standing drinks in the Dutch counties [of New York] was to gather at the bar over a large loving cup compounded with Schiedam, and to pass it right to left down the line. Then, also from right to left, each man would replenish the cup until each had both bought and drunk a full one.
>
> Considering that Matt [Martin Van Buren] covered as many as a dozen taverns a day, his capacity seems to have been all that was said of it, and for that alone he unquestionably deserved his brother's vacated office of Surrogate Judge.

SOME TALL ORDERS

For a little man, Van Buren placed some rather big orders for alcohol. In his defense, he entertained fairly often, so he certainly was not consuming all of it himself. For example, in 1819, Van Buren wrote to Jesse Holt (a lawyer he knew from Albany), asking his friend to secure a sizeable wine order on his behalf. "I want," wrote the future president, "about fifteen or twenty gallons of table wine—say prime Sicily, Madeira, or some other pleasant, but light and low wine to drink with dinner. I wish that you would get Mr. Duer, who takes this, to select it for me, and buy and send it up. Get me also a box of good raisins and a basket of good figs, and send them with the wine."

When he served as ambassador to England (1831–1833), Van Buren felt he needed an adequate supply of the best champagne but ordered cheaper clarets and other wines to get him through less important social visits or gatherings.

Once he retired to Lindenwald, Van Buren—as an ex-president—still felt the need to entertain with a high level of hospitality. That meant multiple dinner courses, properly accompanied by vintages of reasonable merit. As visitor Richard B. Gooch remarked on one such visit to Van Buren's homestead: "There were a dozen courses with wines and champagne. After dinner, liqueurs and brandy were served in the drawing room."

GOUT GUYS

Van Buren and James Buchanan both loved to drink, and they both paid for it in later life. Both men suffered from gout, a disease that is often associated with overindulgence in alcohol and rich food. Van Buren relished oysters and wine, for example—both on the "no-no" list for those suffering from gout.

Van Buren was a prime candidate for gout, as he exercised little (fishing was one of his few activities) and often either attended or hosted lavish dinners. By the 1840s, a visitor to Lindenwald wrote home to a relative, stating: "Van Buren has gotten fat." The former president was, of course, retired at that point, with little hope of a political comeback—although he did run halfheartedly as the Free Soil (anti-slavery) candidate in 1848, managing just ten percent of the vote in the election won by General Zachary Taylor, Whig and slave-owner.

Suffering from the disease in the last decade of his life, Van Buren journeyed to some health spas in search of relief—including the famed French resort at Aix-Les-Baines, Savoy, in 1854. But Van Buren did not cut back on his favorite wines, and other alcohol was readily available at Lindenwald.

LAST CALL

Late in his life, "The Fox of Kinderhook" hosted New Year's Day festivities at his homestead in 1861. Bottles of wine, Schiedam, and a lemonade punch laced with Burgundy were featured beverages at the bash.

POLK

★ 1845–1849 ★

"GREAT CONFUSION, I LEARNED, PREVAILED IN BOTH HOUSES DURING THIS NIGHT'S SESSION AND WHAT IS DEEPLY TO BE REGRETTED SEVERAL MEMBERS AS I WAS INFORMED WERE EXCITED BY DRINK."

—James K. Polk

DRUNK ON
DESTINY

I F JAMES K. POLK, the eleventh president of the United States, was ever drunk on anything, it probably was the concept of "Manifest Destiny"—the brash idea that the United States would one day stretch from "sea to shining sea," and with God's blessing, to boot.

Polk was the original "dark horse" candidate; he won the Democratic nomination for president on the ninth ballot by outmaneuvering such political heavyweights as Lewis Cass of Michigan and former president Martin Van Buren. Polk then beat Kentucky's Henry Clay, the Whig Party candidate, in the election of 1844. His victory brought joy to an aging Andrew Jackson, who long considered Polk his protégé (one of JKP's nicknames was "Young Hickory") and Clay his mortal enemy.

In the 1950s, a brand of whiskey marketed under the Old Crow brand ran a series of historically themed advertisements. Some depicted a snow-haired Andrew Jackson drinking bourbon with various notables of the pre–Civil War age, including James K. Polk. But if Polk drank any whiskey, it seems unlikely that he took anything more than social sips.

Polk rarely drank, but he lived in an era when many famous pols were hard liquor drinkers. Men such as Sam Houston, Daniel Webster, and his rival Henry Clay—not to mention his role model, Jackson—all were imbibers. That fact sometimes made Polk's political life more complicated.

BOOZE FOR THE VOTERS

With his Presbyterian upbringing, James Polk was well versed in the pitfalls of Demon Alcohol and, therefore, avoided it in excess. But Polk the politician also knew the merits and necessity of the stuff. Supplying liquid refreshment to your would-be constituents was by no means a new concept—indeed, it predated the United States; George Washington supplied liquor to his voting block in colonial Virginia.

Running for a seat in the Tennessee state legislature in 1823, Polk's campaign purchased more than twenty gallons of hard cider, whiskey, and brandy to woo voters. Polk won handily, but apparently the liquid assistance ignited some rough-and-tumble confrontations on election day, since the other side utilized similar alcoholic tactics.

> ... Polk's campaign purchased more than twenty gallons of hard cider, whiskey, and brandy to woo voters.

When Polk ran for governor of Tennessee in 1838 (which he also won), he gave a speech in Murfreesboro; and judging by the description of the festive aftermath, it was clear election tactics had not changed dramatically. According to some accounts, the pro-Polk crowd devoured forty sheep, forty piglets, six beeves, hundreds of pounds of ham, bread, and vegetables, and then guzzled "the generous juice of the grape, whiskey, and cognac" to put an exclamation point on the outing.

DEFENDING "BIG DRUNK"

As one of President Andrew Jackson's most trusted allies, Polk fought battles on Old Hickory's behalf while serving in the Senate. Some of those battles were more winnable than others.

One big problem (for both Jackson and Polk) was Sam Houston, the future president of Texas. In the early 1830s, Houston was something of a thin-skinned brute with a hair-trigger temper and a weakness for alcohol. In fact, Houston had been nicknamed "Big Drunk" by the Cherokee tribe with which he had once resided.

In April 1832, an Ohio congressman named William Stanbery insinuated—on the floor of the House—that Houston had been involved in a shady deal (concerning bids on food rations to Indian tribes forcibly removed to the West) with other members of Jackson's administration. Infuriated, the future hero of Texas wanted to smash Stanbery on the spot. But Polk hastily intervened and steered the belligerent Houston outside to cool off.

Polk only delayed the inevitable, however. Several weeks later, Houston identified Stanbery on a Washington street. Bellowing that the Ohioan was a "damn rascal," Houston began to throttle him with a sizeable cane carved out of hickory. Stanbery attempted to shoot Houston, but his pistol misfired. With Stanbery convalescing from his beating, Congress arrested Houston (who was represented in court by lawyer Francis Scott Key of "Star-Spangled Banner" fame). But Polk used his influence and persuasive oratory to water down the punishment. Houston was fined a hefty five hundred dollars, but he skipped off to Texas (and his ultimate destiny of defeating Santa Anna at the Battle of San Jacinto) without ever paying up.

Houston later admitted that, on the night before his summons before Congress, he and many of his powerful friends (some of whom were supposed to pass judgment on Houston the next day) had downed lots of liquor in Houston's hotel room. As Houston himself related:

> We sat late and you may judge how we drank when I tell you that Stevenson [Andrew Stevenson, the Speaker of the House] at midnight was sleeping on the lounge. [Colonel] Baylie Peyton was out of commission and gone to his room and [Tennessee Senator] Felix Grundy had ceased to be interesting.

A MEXICAN-AMERICAN TOAST

Polk is known as one of the most successful presidents in terms of achieving the goals he set on his one-term agenda. Among his greatest accomplishments was winning the Mexican-American War and seizing virtually the entire Southwest from Mexico. As a tribute to this legacy, Polk's cocktail is the Mexicana, a refreshing tequila-based concoction.

Mexicana

1½ oz. tequila
1 oz. lemon juice
½ oz. pineapple juice
1 tsp. grenadine or pomegranate syrup

Pour all ingredients into a cocktail shaker three-quarters full of ice. Shake vigorously and strain into a cocktail glass.

But Houston (who once jested that Polk's problem was that "he drank too much water") confirmed Young Hickory's reputation for moderation, adding: "Polk rarely indulged and left us early."

THE BASKET OF BUBBLY BET

James K. Polk was serious, hardworking (perhaps to a fault; those closest to Polk worried that he wore himself down), and pragmatic. But Polk did enjoy keeping James Buchanan, his secretary of state, a bit off balance. Polk once called out Buchanan on his wording in a diplomatic document. As Polk recounted in his diary:

> He insisted that he was right. I then jocosely said to him, I will stand you a basket of champaign [sic] that this letter is not in the usual form as you insist.... He promptly said, Done, I take you up, and rising in fine humour went out.

When Buchanan came back, he was still brimming with confidence. He was armed with a book that he felt certain contained an example in which just such a document had previously been worded. But after quite some time searching, Buchanan's mood faded to one of resignation, as Polk noted:

> He seemed to be disappointed & said, Well, if I don't find such a precedent today I will send you the basket of champaign [sic]. I smiled and told him I would not accept it, and that I had been jesting when I proposed [it], and had done so only to express in an earnest manner my conviction that I was right. But, he said, if I had won it I would have made you pay it, & I will pay it to you.

Polk again refused to accept the champagne. His "victory" (in addition to successfully "tweaking" Buchanan's ego) seemed also to be a refresher course in leadership skills. Polk finished the anecdote in his diary with: "I record this incident for the purpose of showing how necessary it is for me to give my vigilant attention even to the form & details of my [subordinates'] duties."

POLK'S EXECUTIVE MANSION PARTIES

First lady Sarah Polk banned hard liquor (such as whiskey) and dancing at official Executive Mansion receptions. Wine, champagne, and brandy were served, however. One wonders whether her husband, always a nose-to-the-grindstone kind of public servant, would have noticed one way or the other. Consider his diary entry of Friday, November 13, 1846:

> This was reception evening, but being much engaged in my office, I did not go into the parlour. I learn from the family that quite a number of persons, ladies & gentlemen called.

Sometimes, in fact, if the president happened to be busy working, Sarah Polk would host receptions without her husband.

BELLIGERENT BENTON

Not all of President Polk's visitors qualified as gentlemen. In Polk's time, it was relatively easy for someone to walk in the door of the Executive Mansion and wait in line to make some request for a political or military appointment. These men were typically called "office seekers," and Polk's diaries are laced with derogatory comments about bothersome callers of this ilk.

To make matters worse, not all of these office seekers were sober, or, in some cases, sane. Security around the president—particularly in a pre-Lincoln era—was surprisingly lax. As Polk recorded in his diary (on October 25, 1847), one Monday an excitable young man burst into his office demanding an appointment in the army, at the rank of lieutenant, no less.

The situation was complicated by the fact that the man was John Randolph Benton, the son of powerful senator Thomas Hart Benton, known for his volatile temper. In younger days, the elder Benton had brawled in a Nashville tavern with Andrew Jackson, leaving a non-lethal bullet in Old Hickory's frame—something of a permanent souvenir. Polk would have been well aware of this scandalous story.

Polk ("in a mild tone") told him there were no openings, and, if there were openings, his inclination would be to consider men already serving in the Mexican-American War and promote through the ranks. In short, Polk said he could not promise his brash visitor anything. He wrote:

> He left my office in quite a passion, & very rudely, swearing profanely as he went [out] the door. In a loud and boisterous tone…. "By God" he would do something, but I lost the remaining words that he uttered…. Mr. Arthur of Baltimore, who was present, said he smelt liquor on his breath & thought he was drunk. All present expressed their amazement at his conduct.

THE DEVIL AND DANIEL WEBSTER

Intoxicated office seekers were not the only men who made President Polk's life miserable. Congress was notorious for allowing drinking to go on, even during important votes. The drinkers included even Daniel Webster, arguably the most esteemed orator of his day, though some claimed his flow of eloquence was directly proportional to the amount of liquor he consumed.

Congress was notorious for allowing drinking to go on, even during important votes.

One can almost sense the temperate disgust as Polk remarks in his diary on August 9, 1846, about the "disreputable scene":

> Great confusion, I learned, prevailed in both Houses during this night's Session and what is deeply to be regretted several members as I was informed were excited by drink. Among others I was informed that Senators Webster & Barrow [Alexander Barrow of Louisiana] were quite drunk, so much so that the latter gentleman, it was said, was noisy and troublesome.

LAST CALL ....

"Blacksmith Harry"—a slave on one of Polk's plantations—claimed in a letter to have won "40 gallons of whiskey" betting that Polk would win the presidency. He assured Polk that he had no intention of drinking it all himself.

FRANKLIN

PIERCE

★ 1853–1857 ★

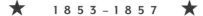

"WHAT CAN AN EX-PRESIDENT OF THE
UNITED STATES DO EXCEPT GET DRUNK?"

—Franklin Pierce

A DARK HORSE DRINKER

THE HARD-DRINKING British prime minister Sir Winston Churchill once boasted (not without reason): "I have taken more out of alcohol than it has taken out of me." But Franklin Pierce, the fourteenth president of the United States, could never have made such an outrageous claim. Drinking destroyed Pierce's health and damaged both his public and political image.

One could argue that Pierce had reason to drink, certainly more than most men. Besides the fact that his personal life was marked by tragedy, Pierce was also trapped in the middle of the nation's major controversy: slavery. His story is thus something of a sobering chapter in the history of presidential drinking.

Despite his New Hampshire roots, Pierce was that rare Northerner sympathetic to the South and that region's insistence on continuing—or even expanding—slavery. As Pierce (a dark horse Democrat selected on the forty-ninth ballot) prepared to become president, he proclaimed: "I believe that involuntary servitude, as it exists in different States of this Confederacy, is recognized by the Constitution."

The Whigs and abolitionists branded Pierce a "doughface"—a term of derision directed toward Northerners siding with the South on this explosive issue. That label haunted him until his final days.

BOWDOIN BOY

Pierce's father Benjamin was a Revolutionary War hero who fought at the Battle of Bunker Hill. Benjamin eventually was elected governor of New Hampshire, although his Federalist adversaries labeled him a profane tavern-owner who swilled much of the liquor he sold. Though not wealthy, the family was able to send young Frank (just fifteen when he first arrived) to Bowdoin College in Maine.

At Bowdoin, Pierce made some lifelong friends, including Nathaniel Hawthorne, destined to become one of the country's most renowned writers. Hawthorne enjoyed hunkering down at Ward's Tavern, a rustic watering hole near the Bowdoin campus, drinking wine and playing cards. In fact, Hawthorne was sometimes fined for drinking and gambling. Frank Pierce managed to dodge those bullets, but he did pick up some college fines for skipping church services. But in all likelihood, Pierce—an athletic, engaging, and good-looking young student (he later acquired the sobriquet "Handsome Frank")—imbibed with his college friends at a very early age.

BAD COMPANY

Like most of the early U.S. presidents, Pierce pursued law as a career before venturing into the political arena. Riding the Jacksonian Democratic wave, Pierce won a congressional seat and arrived in Washington, D.C., in 1832, as Old Hickory began his second term. Not yet thirty, the poised and well-spoken Pierce showed great promise.

The nation's capital was a backwater swamp in those days; unhealthy is some obvious ways (a hotbed for "bilious fever" and other diseases) as well as some insidious ones. Still unmarried at the time, Pierce ran around with other unfettered congressmen, many of whom were no strangers to drinking, gambling, and chasing women.

Pierce, in fact, did not let party lines stop him from socializing, as he even accepted the top-shelf hospitality of Senator Daniel Webster, the older Whig (and notorious drinker) from Massachusetts.

When a fellow Democrat tried to caution Pierce about socializing with the enemy, the congressman made it clear that he would make his own decisions.

THE WILLARD

At the hub of it all was the Willard Hotel. There were hundreds of establishments in the capital, of course, but the Willard was the center of Washington's social beehive. And liquor made that beehive buzz.

> ...the Willard was the center of Washington's social beehive. And liquor made that beehive buzz.

As Hawthorne—Pierce's old friend and first biographer—once advised in an *Atlantic Monthly* article:

> Adopt the universal habit of the place, and call for a mint julep, a whiskey skin, a gin cock-tail, a brandy smash or a glass of pure Old Rye, for the conviviality of Washington sets in at an early hour and, so far I had an opportunity of observing, never terminates at any hour.

DRUNKEN THEATRICS

Pierce married Jane Appleton, the daughter of Bowdoin College president Jesse Appleton, in 1834. Jane was quite reserved, a nondrinker, and not very sociable. She despised Washington, D.C., so the young congressman Pierce spent most of his time in the capital alone.

The culture of the U.S. Congress at that time was definitely a drinking one; some members drank openly on the floor. Pierce—who had the twin misfortune of liking alcohol and lacking an ability to handle it well—did not always pick the best companions.

THE POPULAR SMASH

One of Pierce's college buddies, author Nathanial Hawthorne, once wrote about how the bar of the Willard Hotel was the center of the Washington social scene. He then proceeded to list the most popular drinks of the day. Among them was the Brandy Smash. While similar to the mint julep, the brandy and additional garnishes give it a flavor all its own.

The Brandy Smash
1 sugar cube
1 oz. club soda
5 mint leaves
2 oz. brandy
1 orange slice and 1 cherry for garnish

Combine the sugar cube, club soda, and mint leaves in the bottom of an old fashioned glass. Muddle moderately. Add ice cubes and brandy. Stir gently and garnish with the orange and cherry.

One of Pierce's worst acquaintances was Edward Hannegan, a U.S. representative (and later U.S. senator) from Indiana. Hannegan was a heavy boozer who, when intoxicated, had a penchant for violence.

In February 1836, Pierce, Hannegan, and future governor of Virginia Henry A. Wise—all intoxicated—arrived at a Washington theater. Apparently the tipsy trio was placed in the same box as an army officer who had a "history" with Hannegan, and a tumultuous confrontation soon ensued, with the short-tempered and boozed-up Hannegan yanking out his pistol. Others intervened to stop any further violence, and the military man was transferred out of the city before a duel could be arranged.

Shortly after that incident, Pierce became very ill with pleurisy. It took him weeks to recover. But it was five years before the future president attempted to quit drinking—a sound decision, but not a lasting one.

PIERCE AND "THE PLEDGE"

Pierce won the New Hampshire U.S. Senate seat in 1837 and returned to Washington. But he only managed to break from alcohol when he left the capital city. He resigned from the Senate in 1841 and returned to the Granite State. For the first time in years, he seemingly enjoyed long stretches of sobriety. He also tackled strenuous work on the family farm.

In that time period, Pierce felt confident enough to write his brother-in-law, stating:

> I am now in strong and robust health. I take daily a great deal of exercise… have not used a particle of tobacco in any shape or taken anything more than black tea & that only in the morning since I got settled here.

Amazingly, Pierce actually signed the temperance pledge. He also pushed to abolish the "using and vending of liquor" within

Concord (the New Hampshire capital) city limits in 1843. Clearly, when Pierce receded from politics he also took a step back from the abyss of alcoholism.

SOUTH OF THE BORDER

When the Mexican-American War commenced in 1845, Pierce wanted in on the action, although many New Englanders opposed what they termed "Mr. Polk's War." His connections trumped his lack of military experience, and he soon rose to the rank of brevet colonel.

Pierce drifted back to his old habits. Boredom, in its own sneaky way, proved nearly as dangerous as the battlefield. Colonel Pierce (his temperance pledge seemingly forgotten) helped form the "Aztec Club"—essentially a place where officers could hobnob, drink liquor, and gamble.

Once again, Pierce was involved in a potentially fatal incident involving drinking. When one officer accused another one of cheating in a card game, Pierce intervened. The accusing officer made threats and claimed that only Pierce's advanced rank prevented him from challenging him to a duel. The next day, however, sober minds prevailed—apologies were made and accepted—and, with the war coming to an end, the soldiers soon left Mexico for home.

FORNEY'S FORECAST

Pierce, nicknamed "Young Hickory of the Granite Hills," won the 1852 presidential election over Whig general Winfield Scott, crushing "Old Fuss and Feathers" in the electoral vote 254 to 42.

As Pierce traveled to Washington to begin his presidency in 1853, John W. Forney sent a rather disturbing letter to his friend (and future president) James Buchanan. As a newspaperman, Forney was no stranger to hard drinkers and could hold his own in those ranks himself. But even Forney was taken aback by Pierce's vulnerability to alcohol and did not mince his words when writing to Buchanan:

Pierce has had a fine reception but I deeply, deeply deplore his habits. He drinks deep. My heart bleeds for him for he is a gallant and a generous spirit. The place overshadows him. He is crushed by its great duties.... His experience convinces me that a great mistake was made in putting him in at all.

Forney was right to be concerned. Although Pierce periodically quit drinking, his natural inclination to be social (and perhaps a need to dull the tragedies of his life, including his son's recent death) always brought Pierce back to alcohol.

LAST CALL ....

When his party failed to support him for reelection in 1856, Pierce allegedly was heard to say: "What can an ex-President of the United States do except get drunk?" (There are other versions of the line that are quite similar.)

Did Pierce really say that? Perhaps. His major biographers do not reference it, but the line nevertheless has been widely circulated. It may be just another presidential myth—though perhaps Pierce said something close to that, if only in jest.

JAMES

BUCHANAN

★ 1857–1861 ★

"IN ORDER TO BE CONSIDERED A CLEVER AND SPIRITED
YOUTH, I ENGAGED IN EVERY SORT OF EXTRAVAGANCE
AND MISCHIEF."

—James Buchanan

OLD BUCK

SHORTLY AFTER James Buchanan's death on June 1, 1868, a Lancaster, Pennsylvania, newspaper published some of his final thoughts. One of the fifteenth president's more defensive proclamations was: "I have no regret for any public act of my life and history will vindicate my memory from every unjust aspersion."

History, however, did not share Buchanan's enthusiasm. Pennsylvania's only president is typically rated as one of America's worst—cited as timid and indecisive in the face of the rebellion and the 1861 siege against Fort Sumter, leaving incoming president Lincoln to clean up the mess.

But if Buchanan—nicknamed "Old Buck"—was uncertain during a national emergency, he was on quite a familiar battlefield when it came to jousting with Demon Alcohol. He began drinking in his mid-teens and kept at it late into life, until complications from gout forced him to reluctantly wave the white flag.

Buchanan was renowned among his contemporaries for his ability to handle large quantities of wine or whiskey without showing the usual telltale effects of intoxication. He also had a taste for the top-shelf stuff and had no qualms about providing champagne and other quality wines for lavish dinner parties or celebrations. In contrast to his marks as a leader, "Old Buck" warranted straight A's when it came to his ability to handle alcohol.

WELL TOASTED

James Buchanan had a collegiate reputation for "spirited" rambunctiousness. As a student at Dickinson College, Buchanan drank all sixteen toasts proposed at a Fourth of July gathering in 1808, and presumably indulged in some extra "salutes" as well. The young "Buck" (only sixteen when he began college) was something of a loose cannon at the Carlisle, Pennsylvania, college. He apparently defied institutional rules by smoking cigars and incurring various infractions when he went into town.

Admittedly, there were plenty of bad influences. Jeremiah Atwater, the principal of Dickinson College, complained that "Drunkenness, swearing, lewdness & dueling" held considerable sway over the student body. Some of Buchanan's misdeeds might have been the result of peer pressure, as he once admitted that "in order to be considered a clever and spirited youth, I engaged in every sort of extravagance and mischief."

In addition, Buchanan, although obviously bright, was regarded as somewhat arrogant by his professors. In fact, the college suspended him for disorderly conduct at one point, and the future president—"mortified"—had to pull strings to be reinstated. Although he secured a second chance, Buchanan nevertheless felt snubbed when the college recognized another student, instead of him, as its outstanding scholar.

Proof that he never really forgave the college for that slight was evident decades later when Buchanan retired to his beloved Wheatland. When Dickinson representatives wrote to him requesting a hefty donation to endow a professorship, the former president dismissively replied: "The world is greatly mistaken as to the amount of my fortune."

A SPIRITED VARIETY

Buchanan tried—and liked—many kinds of alcohol, especially as a young lawyer and international diplomat. He often frequented the Grape Tavern in Lancaster. He obviously loved a variety of wines, from champagne to Madeira, one of his dependable favorites.

> There I sinned very much in the article of
> hot whiskey toddy which they term punch.
> The Irish women are delightful.

In fact, Buchanan's letters from his time as a diplomat in Russia and as a European traveler speak to his willingness to sample whatever the drink of the land happened to be. From Russia (he served as an ambassador there under President Jackson from 1832–1833) he wrote his friend John Reynolds that the royalty drank less than he expected. As for the working classes, Buchanan said: "The peasants are jolly, good-natured fellows who drive furiously and seem happy. They are rogues, nevertheless."

But Buchanan also noted, perhaps not without a tinge of admiration, that the common Russian "rogue" consumed "a species of hot white brandy enough to kill the Devil." One must assume that he was referring Russian vodka.

When his mission in Russia was completed, Buchanan was anxious to return to America and resume his political career. But he also took time to travel down the Rhine River and to the Buchanan ancestral home in the north of Ireland. As he journeyed down the Rhine, drifting past its famous castles, Buchanan remarked: "I felt a little romantic in descending the Rhine... I never took much to the Rhenish until I got into its native country. There I acclimated to it & now feel that the taste will accompany me through life. But I have some talent in that line."

With Buchanan, it might be a coin-flip to guess whether he was referring to the famous white wines of the region (often referred to as "Rhenish") or the Rhine River culture in general. From Ireland, Buchanan gleefully wrote to Reynolds: "There I sinned very much in the article of hot whiskey toddy which they term punch. The Irish women are delightful."

The latter statement about the Irish women seems to fly in the face of the persistent rumor that Buchanan was gay (in the modern sense of that word, and not, as one of his early biographers

A BRONX FOR BUCHANAN

Buchanan is the only U.S. president born in Pennsylvania. And to commemorate the Quaker State, here's a cocktail invented in Philadelphia, but made famous elsewhere. The Bronx is named for the restaurant where it became famous in neighboring New York.

The Bronx

2 oz. gin
½ oz. sweet vermouth
½ oz. dry vermouth
1 oz. orange juice
Orange twist for garnish

Pour all ingredients into a shaker three-quarters full of ice cubes. Shake well and strain into a chilled cocktail glass. Add the orange twist.

innocently referred to him, as "a gay bachelor with a flair for society"). The rumors persist because he never married and also because he apparently shared lodgings for more than fifteen years in Washington with Georgia senator William Rufus King prior to becoming president. What letters that survive between Buchanan and King reflect an extremely close friendship, but nothing that proves there was a sexual relationship. Buchanan was briefly engaged early in life, but it ended in tragedy; when the engagement was broken off (for reasons never quite clear), his fiancée seemingly went to pieces and died just days later.

Since Buchanan never married, the role of first lady fell to his niece, a charming and capable woman named Harriet Lane. While one might be tempted to debate Buchanan's sexual inclinations, there is nothing ambiguous about Old Buck's attraction to whiskey, wine, and other liquors; the record shows that he consistently enjoyed his libations.

THE BUCHANAN BASH

In January 1846, then secretary of state Buchanan hosted what could be called (in modern terms) "a bash" at Carusi's Saloon, the premier watering hole in Washington at the time. Presumably there must have been quite a few guests and most of them thirsty ones, as the tally for what was consumed included three hundred bottles of wine, one hundred and fifty bottles of champagne, and liquor for hard-core drinkers.

The alcohol washed down some rich dinner selections prepared by the French chef Gautier. The menu included some modern-day mainstays such as ham, turkey, beef, and lobster. as well as some wild entrees abundant in Buchanan's era, such as venison and pheasant.

FORNEY'S REVELATIONS

John Forney was at one time Buchanan's political manager and a major cog in Old Buck's 1856 ascension to the Executive Mansion. He once gave a rather eye-opening "rundown" of the fifteenth president's drinking prowess. This litany of Buchanan's ability to quaff massive amounts of liquor, with seemingly mild effect, was printed in Forney's own *Philadelphia Press* as Old Buck's presidential term was coming to a merciful close.

Leaving room for embellishment, Forney—a man definitely accustomed to hoisting a glass himself—colorfully remarked: "The Madeira and sherry that he has consumed would fill more than one old cellar, and the rye whiskey that he has 'punished' would make Jacob Baer's heart glad." (Jacob Baer was a well-known whiskey merchant in Washington, D.C.)

> The Madeira and sherry that he has consumed would fill more than one old cellar.

Forney furthermore stated that Buchanan sometimes coupled a Sunday trip to church with a stop at Baer's to pick up a cask of "old J. B." whiskey, which he liked both for its quality and the fact that the initials matched his own.

And woe to the spirited fellow who felt he could keep pace with Buchanan; Forney claimed it was a dangerous contest against a man of such experience. Why Forney was so forthcoming on his former boss's ability to consume alcohol is a question worth pondering. Although they had once been fast friends (Forney, like Buchanan, had roots in Lancaster), they were drifting toward estrangement by 1860—partly over the issue of slavery and perhaps also because Buchanan had not offered Forney a position in his administration that Forney felt was worth taking. Forney eventually became a major supporter of Abe Lincoln—with enough zeal that Lincoln's foes sneeringly referred to him as "Lincoln's dog."

THE PROHIBITION PROBE

There is a tendency to think of the Prohibition movement as a product of the early twentieth century. But its peculiar sentiments were stirring even back in Buchanan's day. And while Buchanan may have been wishy-washy on the major issues of his era, he felt sure Prohibition was a fool's errand. "In [Prohibition], I think, they will entirely fail," he wrote in an 1867 letter. "Lager beer, especially among the Germans, and old rye will be too strong for them. Still, intemperance is a great curse to our people, but it will never be put down by laws prohibiting the sale of all intoxicating liquors...."

The subject of intemperance must have been a curious one for Buchanan to ponder, since the "Sage of Wheatland" himself had such a knack for knocking back alcohol.

OLD BUCK AND THE BEE

Buchanan's own strategy when it came to the emerging forces of temperance seemed to be quite simple: ignore them and pour another drink.

As related in Forney's *Anecdotes of Public Men*, a fuming Pennsylvania judge once charged into then senator Buchanan's office about the judge's harsh treatment in a temperance publication called *The Bee*.

> I [Forney] was sitting with Mr. Buchanan when the irate Judge came in with *The Bee* in his hand. He was a warm friend of the Pennsylvania Senator; and when the latter said, "Won't you take a glass of wine with us, sir?" he said, "I thank you sir, but I came to show you this terrible article against my opinion in *The Bee*." "The what?" said Old Buck, then a very handsome bachelor of fifty. "*The Bee*, sir, said the little Judge in high anger. "And where the Devil is *The Bee* printed, Judge?" "Why Mr. Buchanan, it is printed in this very town, and has a very large circulation among the temperance people and it has given me much pain by its censure of my judicial action, and, by God, sir, I intend to take notice of it from the bench tomorrow!"
>
> These words were uttered with much feeling. The honest and sensitive jurist had been stung to the quick

by the little *Bee*, but I shall never forget Buchanan's words as he pushed a cold, bright glass of "Old Wanderer" Madeira to his judicial friend:

"Let me have the honor of a glass of wine with you, sir. I declare to you that I have never to this day heard of the paper you call *The Bee*; but you have made a good record as an honest and impartial judge, and you will be remembered for this long after the name of that paper is forgotten. The faithful public man who feels that he is right, must accept criticism, but he will outlive it as sure as the both of us must die."

DOWN AND GOUT

Buchanan expressed some brief reluctance about running for president due to some minor health issues. He was already in his mid-sixties when he took office. Letters from Buchanan's post–Executive Mansion years are increasingly laced with references to gout—a disease that's painful to the joints and inflamed by a diet of rich foods and too much alcohol.

One of Buchanan's last letters, written to his niece, laments that he attended a lavish dinner at a New Jersey shore resort but felt in an "awkward situation" because he was unable "to drink a drop of wine." His frequent flare-ups of gout might well have been the reason.

LAST CALL ....

Buchanan allegedly once admonished a wine merchant for sending small bottles of champagne to the Executive Mansion; Old Buck made it clear that big bottles would be required in the future.

ANDREW

JOHNSON

★ 1865–1869 ★

"IT IS VERY STRANGE THAT SOME MEN WILL
BE ABUSED LIKE THE DEVIL FOR DRINKING A GLASS
OF WHISKEY AND WATER, WHILE OTHERS...
MAY ALMOST ROLL IN THE GUTTERS, AND NOT A
WORD IS SAID ABOUT IT."

—Andrew Johnson

INEBRIATED
AND IMPEACHED

ANDREW JOHNSON, the seventeenth president of the United States, is notorious for two incidents: his inebriated state during his inauguration ceremony for vice president in 1865, and his impeachment by the House of Representatives (and narrow escape in the Senate) in 1868. His political career somehow survived both, but his legacy was tarnished.

Of course, nobody ever really expected Johnson to be president. It took Lincoln's assassination at Ford's Theatre and the failure of John Wilkes Booth's fellow conspirators to kill the vice president for that to happen.

Johnson grew up impoverished in North Carolina and was laboring as a tailor in Tennessee when he grasped a rising political opportunity. He is one of history's most complicated studies: he was, like most presidents before him, a slave-owner, though he eventually emancipated those he owned. He was a man with Southern roots, but a staunch Unionist and a bitter critic of the Dixie aristocrats, whom he felt riled up the average man for secession behind the guise of "states' rights." And though a Democrat in the Jacksonian mold, Johnson was chosen to be running mate of Lincoln—the great Republican.

Those who enjoy perusing the rankings of presidents will typically find Johnson near the bottom of the list. Most of his biographers believe Johnson was a moderate drinker for his era (the inauguration fiasco being an exception). Yet, his political enemies occasionally referred to him as "the drunken tailor."

VP ME!

Abraham Lincoln was disappointed with Hannibal Hamlin, his first vice president. With the 1864 reelection campaign looming, Andrew Johnson emerged from the pack of potential replacement running mates with minimal fanfare. He was given high marks for loyalty when as military governor of Tennessee he withstood a virtual firestorm by siding with the Union, even as his state had thrown its lot in with the Confederacy. Lincoln and Johnson actually ran as the National Union Party ticket.

Lincoln won reelection handily over Democratic nominee General George B. McClellan, whom he'd unceremoniously sacked from command earlier in the war. Johnson, of course, rode Abe's long coattails. But as the inauguration approached, Johnson was quite sick (possibly with typhoid fever), and he alerted Lincoln that, given the unfortunate circumstances, he would

> When Johnson hit town, he got drunk and stayed that way for a day and a half.

prefer not to travel to Washington and deal with the inauguration ceremonies.

But Lincoln would not hear of it. The commander in chief felt it was important that Johnson be on hand for the occasion. So Johnson reluctantly agreed to make the trip to the capital. It might be a historical toss-up whether Lincoln or Johnson regretted the results of this decision more. That's because when Johnson hit town, he got drunk and stayed that way for a day and a half.

THE FORNEY FACTOR

Johnson's first mistake might have been colliding with John Forney. Forney—then secretary of the Senate—was a newspaper editor, writer, and political operative who had helped his friend

James Buchanan get elected president in 1856. Forney had had a previous waltz or two with alcohol. (John Hay, Lincoln's secretary, described Forney as dangerously drunk on whiskey the night before Abe's Gettysburg Address, for example.)

Of course, it was not unusual in that era to prescribe whiskey as a treatment for various illnesses, and Johnson—feeling somewhat weak from his sickness and the rigors of travel—attended a party hosted by Forney on the evening before the big day. Whiskey certainly would have been offered to the Tennessean to salute his election, as standard hospitality, and perhaps even in the guise of medical treatment. Johnson apparently did not demur.

When Inauguration Day came, dreary and rainy, it was obvious that whiskey, illness, or both still held sway over Johnson. With his speech looming, Johnson asked outgoing VP Hamlin for an additional dose or two of whiskey. Ousted from the Lincoln ticket, Hamlin—temperate when it came to his own drinking—perhaps was only too happy to comply. In some accounts, brandy is said to have been the liquor provided, though nobody argues much about the result. Johnson, on one of the most important days of his political career, opted for the dubious "hair of the dog" strategy. But sometimes the dog bites back.

GRAVE REVIEWS

The outcome was cringe-worthy. Johnson mumbled words that made little sense but weirdly seemed accusatory in nature. The speech was outlined for approximately five minutes, yet Johnson rambled on much longer. Finally, mercifully—after more than fifteen minutes inside the stuffy Senate building—Johnson got the equivalent of the "Broadway hook." Secretary of the Navy Gideon Welles recapped Johnson's spectacular smashup in his diary:

> The Vice-President elect made a rambling and strange harangue, which was listened to with pain and mortification by all his friends. My impressions were that he was under the influence of stimulants, yet I know not that he drinks.

AN UNIMPEACHABLE DRINK

Johnson shares with Bill Clinton and Donald Trump the dubious distinction of being one of the only three presidents to be impeached by the U.S. House of Representatives (though all three were acquitted by the Senate—Donald Trump twice). To toast this distinction, we offer a cocktail with unimpeachable flavor. In fact, it's the most famous cocktail that could be referred to as "peachy." It's the Fuzzy Navel.

Fuzzy Navel

2 oz. vodka
1 oz. peach schnapps
4 oz. fresh orange juice

Pour all ingredients into a highball glass filled with ice. Stir gently.

And Welles was not alone in his concern, noting:

> [James] Speed, who was on my left, said, "All this is in wretchedly bad taste;" and very soon he said, "The man is certainly deranged." I said to [Secretary of War William] Stanton, who was on my right, "Johnson is either drunk or crazy." Stanton said, "Something is evidently wrong."

Indeed. Something was wrong and that something was too much booze.

> He made a bad slip the other day, but you need not be scared. Andy ain't a drunkard.

Future president Rutherford B. Hayes was in the audience and wrote home to his wife, Lucy, bluntly stating: "It was lucky you did not come to the inauguration. The bad weather and Andy Johnson's disgraceful drunkenness spoiled it."

The newspapers, of course, did not let Johnson's bizarre, whiskey-infused performance go unnoticed, either. The Lincoln administration decided the best possible defense was to play possum: Johnson disappeared for a few weeks, holed up at Francis S. Blair's home.

Lincoln, by now quite experienced at defending his generals (chiefly U. S. Grant) against accusations of drunkenness, tried to reassure his own administrators concerning Johnson. Hugh McCullough, secretary of the Treasury, remembered that President Lincoln assured him several days later that Johnson's behavior was an unfortunate occurrence but not one that likely would be revisited. According to McCullough, Lincoln said: "I have known Andy Johnson for many years; he made a bad slip the other day, but you need not be scared. Andy ain't a drunkard."

THE WHISKEY PAPER TRAIL

Andy Johnson may not have been a drunkard, but neither was he a stranger to whiskey. If one reads through his letters and bills, there is ample evidence that Johnson had a taste for quality whiskey—and was willing to pay good money to get it.

For example, a typical letter to Nashville hotelier Samuel J. Carter (a man who seems to have doubled as Johnson's procurer of whiskey) is this one in August of 1863: "If you have any pure Simple Whiskey that is good send me some of it—I have enough that is not fit for any one to drink, yet it is called [good] by some."

Several days later, Johnson's correspondence included this note from a whiskey supplier:

> Hon. Andrew Johnson
> Sir we Sent you a Demijohn of Robinson Co. Whiskey[.]
> Hoping it will meet with your approval[.]

THE SWING AROUND THE CIRCLE

In 1866, in an effort to build support for his Reconstruction agenda and perhaps boost his own likeability, President Johnson embarked on what was dubbed the "Swing around the Circle" tour. It started reasonably well, but ended badly and—when all was said and done—probably hurt Johnson's image.

Johnson surrounded himself with Civil War heroes—General U. S. Grant (a somewhat reluctant draftee), Admiral David Farragut, and the dashing young cavalryman General George Armstrong Custer. The tour involved banquets at which lavish dinners and numerous toasts were made. Some were held at swanky establishments, such as Delmonico's in New York City.

Fearing that the "Swing" might bolster Johnson's popularity, the abolitionists (who hated the president because they felt he was too lenient on the defeated rebels) began to push back; hecklers soon appeared to badger Johnson at speaking engagements, particularly in the Midwest. Johnson—a pugnacious and stubborn man—eagerly engaged these verbal snipers. The result was a chief executive who looked combative and undignified. And, not surprisingly, the opposition speculated that Johnson must have been drunk to be so belligerent. Though there certainly was drinking on the "Swing," Johnson supporters swore he never overindulged.

Because of his obvious "slip" at the 1865 inauguration, Johnson could never quite dodge his enemies' accusations when it came to drinking. In fact, his most vehement detractors often referred to Johnson as "the drunken tailor"—blasts against both his indulgence of alcohol and his working-class roots.

Somewhat thin-skinned, Johnson insisted that the accusations about his alcohol consumption were grossly overstated and once gave this bristling observation: "It is very strange that some men will be abused like the devil for drinking a glass of whiskey and water, while others... may almost roll in the gutters, and not a word is said about it."

Johnson's enemies—and they were significant in both power and number—soon circled in for the kill. Led by the hard-core abolitionists in 1868, they came incredibly close to ousting Johnson from the Executive Mansion. The House of Representatives did, in fact, impeach Johnson, but the Senate fell short—by one vote—of the needed two-thirds majority.

THE ACQUITTAL TOAST

There is some special justice in the fact that Johnson—in an impromptu ceremony—toasted his dodging of the impeachment bullet not with mineral water or champagne but with whiskey from the Executive Mansion cellar.

There was no better firsthand witness to Johnson's reaction to his acquittal than Executive Mansion bodyguard William Crook. When Senator Edmund Ross of Kansas cast the pivotal vote for acquittal on May 16, 1868, Johnson narrowly escaped the charges of "high crimes and misdemeanors." As Crook recounted:

I ran all the way from the Capitol to the White House. I was young and strong in those days, and I made good time. When I burst into the library where the President sat with Secretary Welles and two other men whom I cannot remember, they were quietly talking....

"Mr. President," I shouted, too crazy with delight to restrain myself, "you are acquitted!"

All rose. I made my way to the President and got hold of his hand. The other men surrounded him, and began to shake his hand. The President responded to their congratulations calmly enough for a moment, and then I saw that tears were rolling down his face. I stared at him; and yet I felt I ought to turn my eyes away.

It was all over in a moment, and Mr. Johnson was ordering some whiskey from the cellar. When it came, he himself poured it into glasses for us, and we all stood up and drank a silent toast. There were some sandwiches on the table; we ate some and then we felt better. In a few minutes came a message of congratulations from Secretary Seward to "my dear friend." By that time the room was full of people and I slipped away.

LAST CALL ....

Seward had two reasons to be happy. There was Johnson's acquittal, of course, but also Seward—an aficionado of fine wines—had bet someone a basket of champagne that Johnson would be cleared.

GROVER

CLEVELAND

★ 1885–1889 ★
★ 1893–1897 ★

"WELL, MY DEAR FELLOW,
WHAT DID YOU EXPECT, CHAMPAGNE?"

—Grover Cleveland

BIG STEVE

ACENTURY BEFORE a sex scandal nearly destroyed Bill Clinton's chances of winning the presidency, Grover Cleveland demonstrated that a presidential candidate could sidestep a serious sex scandal and still reach the Executive Mansion without much manure sticking to his shoes.

In Cleveland's case, the scandal involved his admission that he might have fathered a child out of wedlock with Maria Halpin in 1874. To which the forces of James G. Blaine, the Republican nominee, gleefully trumpeted: "Ma, ma, where's my Pa?" After Cleveland won the 1884 election, his Democratic supporters famously blasted back: "Gone to the White House! Ha, ha, ha!"

If not for William Howard Taft, the "most portly president" designation would be held by Cleveland. Born Stephen Grover Cleveland, "Big Steve" was an early nickname. He later acquired "Uncle Jumbo" as well.

An eager eater of meat chops, beefsteaks, sausages, and cheese, and a renowned pounder of beer (plus other forms of alcohol), Cleveland's daily habits led to his corpulence and poor health in general. He rarely exercised, unless you count fishing and some leisurely hunting—both activities which are suitably accompanied by a flask. A newspaper once speculated that he did not attend the theater because it was a real question whether he could fit in a seat. Even by his first term as president, Cleveland—not yet fifty years old—was already limping around with occasional bouts of gout.

RUM, ROMANISM, AND REBELLION

A fateful remark containing the word "rum" may well have helped Cleveland get elected president in the first place.

As the election of 1884 headed into its final days, the Blaine campaign committed two errors—one major and one minor—that may have tipped the election to underdog Cleveland. The minor error was an extravagant "fat cat" feast at the famed Delmonico's restaurant in Manhattan. Cartoonists had a field day with the so-called "millionaires' dinner," and it allowed the Cleveland camp to tarnish Blaine as the tycoon's candidate.

But the major error unfolded when Blaine attended a meeting of clergymen. During this holy gathering, the Protestant minister Reverend Dr. Samuel Burchard smugly proclaimed: "We don't propose to leave our party and identify with the party whose antecedents are rum, Romanism, and rebellion!"

Blaine did nothing, at least initially, to distance himself from the minister's inflammatory rhetoric—a thinly veiled slap at Irish Catholics—and soon the statement was spread all over New York City and, eventually, beyond.

Cleveland sensed that Burchard's blunder might prove to be a political godsend, relegating the Halpin affair to the backburner of the red-hot stove of political scandal. In a letter to his former law firm partner Wilson S. Bissell a month before the election, Cleveland wrote: "The Catholic question is being treated and so well treated in so many different ways that I shall not be at all surprised if what has been done by the enemy should turn out to my advantage."

And according to most political historians, it did. Irish Catholic voters—some of them having presumably been on the fence prior to Burchard's ill-timed disparagement—flocked to Cleveland's side. Cleveland won New York State, worth thirty-six electoral votes at that time, by fewer than 1,200 votes—and, thereby, won the election 218 to 182 over Blaine.

BEER ME IN BUFFALO

As a young lawyer in Buffalo, New York, Cleveland was a frequent visitor to the various German beer halls and gardens in that

> Big Steve could often be found puffing on a fat cigar and hoisting a sweating mug of cold beer.

city. As author Matthew Algeo noted in his book *The President Is a Sick Man*, Big Steve could often be found puffing on a fat cigar and hoisting a sweating mug of cold beer.

His favorite haunts were Diebold's, Schwabl's, Gillick's, and Louis Goetz's. On hot summer nights, he was likely to be spotted at Schenkelberger's or one of the city's other German beer gardens, where sawdust covered the floor and not too much covered the pretty young fräuleins who kept his stein filled.

Perhaps the best beer story from Cleveland's Buffalo days arose from a challenge he had with his friend Lyman Bass when they faced off for the office of district attorney. Familiar drinking partners, Cleveland and Bass agreed to cut down to a mere four beers a day during the campaign.

But after some days slowly passed, both men began to regret this stringent vow to which they had committed themselves.

Thirst, however, provides great motivation for problem-solving. Both men agreed they would still abide by their four-beer rule—but with one minor adjustment: Cleveland and his friendly rival simply upgraded to a full tankard, essentially doubling the amount of guilt-free brew they could consume.

UNCLE JUMBO'S SECRET OP

Cleveland is the only U.S. president to serve two non-consecutive terms, but rather early in his second stint (1893–1897) he faced a very personal challenge: an operation to remove what doctors suspected might be a cancerous growth inside his mouth. In addition to his affinity for alcohol, Cleveland—like U. S. Grant—loved cigars. It was fearfully probable, then, that

SPICY BEER FOR BIG STEVE

Grover "Big Steve" Cleveland earned his nickname for his girth (he was the second largest president behind William Howard Taft). He achieved this honor for his penchant for copious amounts of beer. Our cocktail for Big Steve is a Mexican creation, combining beer and tomato juice in a sort of beer-y Mary called a Spicy Michelada.

Spicy Michelada
3 tbsp. kosher salt
½ tsp. smoked paprika
¼ tsp. cayenne pepper (if desired)
1 oz. lime juice, plus a lime wedge for garnish
8 oz. Mexican beer
1 tsp. Worcestershire sauce
½ tsp. Tabasco or other hot sauce
½ tsp. soy sauce
Freshly cracked black pepper

Combine the salt, paprika, and cayenne pepper on a plate. Moisten rim well with lime wedge and dip into rimming plate. Fill glass with ice, and set aside. In a shaker half-filled with ice, combine remaining ingredients and stir. Strain into prepared glass and add the lime wedge and fresh pepper.

Cleveland—like Grant (who died early in Cleveland's first term in 1885)—had a cancerous tumor.

On top of trepidations concerning the operation, Cleveland worried what effect the news might have on the nation in general and the economy in particular. The economy—already suffering from the collapse of some railroads, including the prominent Reading Railroad, which had gone bankrupt—was in a weakened state. Any fear about the president's health, Cleveland speculated, could only add to the negative environment.

What transpired was one of presidential history's most audacious cover-ups—described in detail and in spellbinding fashion in Matthew Algeo's *The President Is a Sick Man*. Under the guise of a fishing trip on a friend's yacht, Cleveland arranged for half a dozen doctors to remove the vile growth while floating around in the Long Island Sound for several days and thereby out of the sight of nosy newspaper reporters and a prying public.

One can only imagine Cleveland's consternation in the days and hours just prior to the secret operation. But Algeo records that even these dire circumstances did not keep Cleveland from his usual habits. En route by railcar to his clandestine destination, the president lit up a cigar and ordered a glass of whiskey (then had a second) from the porter. One can assume that these actions were more an effort to calm his nerves than they were acts of defiance or bravado.

As for the operation itself (which took place on a table in the yacht's saloon), it was a success; the tumor was removed, and Cleveland—never the picture of health to begin with—lived another fifteen years. Only one newspaperman managed to dig up the truth, but the Cleveland forces scurried to discredit him. The president had merely been suffering from a bad tooth, said Cleveland's spokesmen, and the public largely bought that explanation.

In something of an ironic display, Big Steve's all-star medical team apparently lit up cigars and brought forth a bottle of whiskey to celebrate the success of their undercover operation on the president of the United States.

THE "FRANKIE" FACTOR

Cleveland modified his bachelor ways after his marriage to the young and attractive Frances Folsom on June 2, 1886. (It was a little weird since Cleveland had known her as a little girl and had been her legal guardian, but that's another story.)

Frances was a fairly devoted supporter of the temperance movement; she rarely drank herself. At her wedding ceremony (she was the first to marry an incumbent president in the Executive Mansion) Frances barely touched her lips to the glass during the champagne toast, while Big Steve knocked his wine straight down. Unlike other first ladies of that era, Frances looked the other way when it came to serving wine at the Executive Mansion.

Frankie (as Cleveland called her) also looked the other way when the president imbibed during his "Goodwill Tour" around the country by railroad in 1887. One stop was in Milwaukee—arguably the beer capital of North America—and in Schlitz Park, no less. Uncle Jumbo certainly would have had some foam on his mustache during the Milwaukee stop.

THE TWAIN ASSESSMENT

Mark Twain and Grover Cleveland both lived in Buffalo around 1870, but the future president was a mere sheriff at that time and, therefore, did not rub social shoulders with the famous writer. Twain, in fact, only lived in Buffalo for about eighteen months. But years later, when Governor Cleveland was the president elect, Twain and Cleveland met, and

> Cleveland drunk is a more valuable asset to this country than the whole batch of the rest of our public men sober.

both men rib-bed the other about why they had not associated during their Buffalo days.

If we are to put any belief in Twain's correspondence, however, we must conclude that the great American author held Big Steve in high esteem. Just days before Cleveland's death at Princeton, New Jersey (June 24, 1908, after suffering a heart attack), Twain wrote to his daughter Jean Clemens:

> Of all our public men of today he stands first in my reverence & admiration, & the next one stands two-hundred-&-twenty-fifth. He is the only statesman we have now... Cleveland drunk is a more valuable asset to this country than the whole batch of the rest of our public men sober. He is high-minded; all his impulses are great & pure & fine. I wish we had another of this sort.

LAST CALL

Cleveland preferred hearty German-American fare to fancy French food. Nevertheless, he inherited Chester Arthur's French chef when he first moved into the Executive Mansion. And so the president once lamented in a letter: "I must go to dinner, but I wish it was a pickled herring, Swiss cheese, and a chop at Louis' [the Goetz Tavern in Buffalo] instead of the French stuff I shall find."

And, of course, Big Steve—given his druthers—would have chased all that tasty grub at Goetz's down with something thirst-quenching—preferably several steins of freshly brewed beer.

WOODROW

WILSON

★ 1913–1921 ★

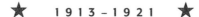

"FRIENDSHIP IS THE ONLY CEMENT THAT WILL EVER
HOLD THE WORLD TOGETHER."

—Woodrow Wilson

PROGRESSIVES
AND PROHIBITION

BORN IN VIRGINIA, Thomas Woodrow Wilson graduated from Princeton University and later became its president. Wilson was serving as the governor of New Jersey when he was swept into the White House in 1912 as the Democratic Party nominee and champion of "progressive" reforms. He defeated Republican incumbent William Howard Taft and former President Theodore Roosevelt (representing the "Bull Moose Party"), plus socialist candidate Eugene Debs.

In his second term, Wilson attempted to keep America out of World War I. But this stance became increasingly impossible to hold, due both to Germany's policy of unrestricted submarine warfare and to hawks in the Senate pushing for U.S. involvement. After the war, Wilson championed the League of Nations, although—much to his lament—the United States itself did not initially join the organization designed to promote understanding and peace.

Some people wrongly think that Wilson must have pushed for Prohibition, since the Eighteenth Amendment (the Volstead Act) was passed during his second term. But, in fact, Wilson vetoed it—only to have Congress override him.

Prior to his veto, Wilson had suffered a serious stroke. Most historians and biographers believe that his second wife, Edith (with assistance from Dr. Cary Grayson) virtually ran the country in Wilson's last years in the White House. Wilson died in 1924 after a more serious stroke at his home on S Street in Washington, D.C.

WILSON—THAT'S ALL!

Wilson made some enemies when he was the president of Princeton University. One of his Princeton faculty foes, Professor Henry Duffield, once claimed that Wilson was "drunk with egotism." Wilson's own words sometimes suggest that he was not eager to embrace compromise, having once stated to an Ivy League audience:

> I am one of those who are of the seed of the indomitable blood, planted in so many parts of the United States, which makes good fighting stuff—the Scotch-Irish. The beauty of a Scotch-Irishman is that he not only thinks he is right, but knows he is right. And I have not departed from the faith of my ancestors.

Neither did Wilson depart from the favorite drink of his ancestors—scotch whisky. Although none of Wilson's opponents, whether academics or politicians, ever claimed he overindulged, the Virginian-born future president was far from a teetotaler. He may have looked like a stodgy academic in his dark suits and top hat—and he was, in fact, our only president with a PhD—but Wilson was a moderate imbiber with a preference for high-quality whisky.

Coincidently, in the early 1900s, there was a popular scotch whisky called "Wilson" (distilled in Baltimore, Maryland, and claiming to date back to 1823), and the product's slogan was: "Wilson—That's all!" The obvious advertising implication being: "If you can have Wilson's whiskey, why ask for anything else?"

Woodrow Wilson's Democratic campaign essentially co-opted this slogan (it was bandied about even when he ran for governor of New Jersey in 1909), and it appeared on campaign posters. "America First" appeared at the top of the poster, above a rather serious-looking portrait of Wilson against a backdrop of the American flag. And below Wilson's picture, in bold letters, appeared: "That's All!"

But the poster was certainly out-done by a jaunty, banjo-strumming campaign song titled—you guessed it—"Wilson, That's All!"

> I think I'll have to drink / To the Democratic cause!

that was played and sung at campaign rallies during Wilson's White House run. The verses brim with references to both Democratic fellowship and alcohol consumption:

> Now convention days are over
> And election time is near
> From East and West, from North to South
> There's just one name in ev'ry mouth
> When a fellow meets a fellow
> And he says to him: "What's yours?"
> He says, "I think I'll have to drink
> To the Democratic cause!"
> It's "Wilson, that's all, Wilson, that's all!"
> Who strikes the public sentiment
> Say who will be our President?
> It's Wilson, that's all
> You'll hear them call, "Tammany, Tammany"
> While on the street or on the car
> While at your home or at the bar
> It's "Wilson, Wilson, Wilson, that's all!"

CHAMPAGNE ON CHAIRS

As the president of Princeton University, Wilson, his first wife Ellen, and their children lived in the prestigious Italianate Victorian mansion called "Prospect House." While Wilson may not have qualified as a "party animal," he certainly knew how to welcome in the New Year.

As the stroke of midnight approached, Wilson gathered everyone in the dining room and filled up the champagne glasses. Then everyone perched themselves on dining room chairs, put one leg up on the table top, and toasted in the new year—while singing the classic Scottish ballad "Auld Lang Syne."

WHISKEY, THAT'S (NOT) ALL!

Woodrow Wilson loved to drink Scotch. And while he may have preferred to drink it straight ("That's all!"), straight whiskey does not make for a very interesting cocktail. So for Woodie's drink, we'll employ his beloved scotch whisky and turn to another famous alliterative name, Rob Roy.

Rob Roy

2 oz. Scotch Whisky

¼ oz. sweet vermouth

dash of angostura bitters

1 maraschino cherry for garnish

Pour all ingredients except the cherry into a shaker two-thirds full of ice. Shake vigorously and strain into a chilled cocktail glass. Add the cherry.

VOLSTEAD VETO

Because Prohibition unfolded during Wilson's presidency, it might be assumed that he approved, or even pushed for, anti-liquor laws in the United States. But Wilson vetoed the Volstead Act, only to be overruled by Congress.

Wilson had attempted a compromise; the war in Europe was ending and with it the need to keep wheat and other grains purely as food sources for soldiers in the field. So when President Wilson addressed the sixty-sixth Congress in 1919, he raised eyebrows by pointing out the obvious:

> The Demobilization of military forces of the country has progressed to such a point that it seems to me entirely safe now to remove the ban upon the manufacture and sale of wines and beers. But I am advised that without further legislation I have not the legal authority to remove the present restrictions.

A backlash came from several directions. A minister from Ohio soon pronounced Wilson's declaration as: "Very unbecoming for an elder in the Presbyterian Church [which Wilson was], and a man holding so high an office as that of President of the United States." Others suspected that German-American brewers were manipulating the White House—and, of course, anti-German sentiment was still running high in the country.

For their part, the "wets" felt Wilson's remarks did not go far enough; they wanted all liquor—not just beer and wine—to be made available to Americans.

SQUIRREL WHISKEY

Like other U.S. presidents, Wilson enjoyed telling stories that featured liquor as a humorous ingredient. One revolved around "squirrel" whiskey.

On December 14, 1910, Wilson gave a speech to the New York Southern Society, staged in the grand ballroom of the Waldorf-Astoria Hotel in Manhattan. William G. McAdoo served as the toastmaster and welcomed Wilson with a lofty prediction: "I invite you, gentlemen, to drink to the health of a future President of the United States."

In return, Wilson regaled the crowd with his tale about squirrel whiskey—which he used to tell the crowd that he was not exactly sure in which direction the future might take him.

> I find myself in one respect (I hope in only one respect), resembling certain individuals I heard of in a story that was repeated to me the other day. A friend of mine in Canada with a fishing party was imprudent enough to sample some whiskey that was called "squirrel" whiskey. It was understood that it was called "squirrel" whiskey because it made those who drank it inclined to climb a tree. This gentleman imbibed too much of this dangerous liquid and the consequence was that when he went to the train to go with the rest of the company, he took a train bound South instead of a train bound North. Wishing to recover him, his companion telegraphed the conductor of the south-bound train: "Send short man named Johnson back for the north-bound train. He is intoxicated." Presently they a got a reply from the conductor: "Further particulars needed; there are thirteen men on the train who don't know either their name or their destination."
>
> ...Now, I am sure that I know my name, but I am not as sure as Mr. McAdoo that I know my destination, and I have at the present so much to do that I don't think I am very concerned where I land....

Wilson unleashed his squirrel whiskey story on several other occasions. The president even regaled British prime minister David Lloyd George with the tale during a brief respite at the Paris Peace Conference in 1919.

DRAWING THE LINE

When Wilson launched his run for governor of New Jersey, a Judge Hudspeth gave him a good-natured warning. "Dr. Wilson," Hudspeth stated, "you need not be surprised that sometime during your trip around the State, some exuberant voter will slap you on the back and say: 'Come, Woody, old man, let's have a drink!'" Wilson responded with a good-natured laugh, allowing: "The intimate introduction is all right, but I would draw the line on liquoring up!"

PEACE TALKS AND PROHIBITION

The summer of 1919 proved to be a hectic one for Woodrow Wilson, wrapping up the Paris Peace Conference in Europe with his trusty friend and personal physician Dr. Cary Grayson, a former admiral, by his side. And the American contingent was well aware that when they arrived home that the United States would, at least officially, be a "dry" country as of July 1.

> The intimate introduction is all right, but I would draw the line on liquoring up!

If Wilson and Grayson had not remembered that Prohibition was indeed looming in the very near future, European leaders were only too pleased to remind them. The day Wilson, British prime minister Dave Lloyd George, and France's Georges Clemenceau signed the controversial Treaty of Versailles in the Hall of Mirrors on June 28, Dr. Grayson wryly noted in his diary:

> Clemenceau had tea served for the party. He also had wine brought in and proposed a toast to the peace and good health of the party. After the toast had been drunk he turned to me and said: "You had better have another one because you will not be able to get any of this (wine) when you get back home."

Wilson was somewhat willing to poke fun at the situation, judging from a discussion (in the spring of 1919) with Lloyd George—one that started out being about sparrows. As Dr. Grayson recorded in his diary:

> The subject turned to birds, particularly the English sparrow. The President said that the English sparrow in America was a menace because it whipped away the thrush, the robin and other songbirds. Lloyd-George was surprised to hear that, because, he said, "it was such a quiet bird at home in England." The President said: "How do you account for the fact that it is so peaceful at home and such a fighter with us?" Lloyd-George said: "I think it is due to the fact that your climate is more energetic; that you have more champagne in the atmosphere." The President said: "That may have held good in the past but it will not hold good now, because we are dry...."

WILSON'S WINE CELLAR

Wilson stocked an impressive wine cellar at the White House. Rather than leave it to the incoming Warren Harding and his cronies (who surely would have guzzled it down in rapid order), Wilson wisely opted to move it to his new residence prior to leaving the White House.

This reasonable request actually required special approval from Congress since it was technically illegal (under the Volstead Act) to transport liquor.

In addition to wine, Wilson liked an occasional sip or two of scotch whisky. In the latter stages of his life—despite the Volstead Act—correspondence signed with Wilson's name appeared to acknowledge his use of scotch whisky to combat the challenges of a serious stroke that left him in a fragile state.

A typical example was a June 14, 1921, letter that Wilson sent to Louis Seibold. (Seibold was a journalist trusted by the Wilson circle; he once conducted an interview intended to show that President Wilson had recovered from his stroke.) The letter read:

> My dear Seibold:
>   The goods arrived as per Grayson's schedule and I am very grateful. You certainly know what is wanted and when.
>   With warmest regards from us all;
>   Faithfully and gratefully,
>   Woodrow Wilson

As Seibold acknowledged in a note to Katharine E. Brand, "the goods" were six bottles of rare scotch whisky, which he passed on to Dr. Grayson for delivery to the former president. At another time, Seibold noted: "I personally delivered to Mister Wilson's house some very good Rhine wine—Berncastler Doctor—as a gift from my father."

LAST CALL

Wilson's vice president, Thomas R. Marshall, is most famous for his quote: "What this country needs is a really good five-cent cigar!"

But Marshall also was a reformed alcoholic who sometimes made speeches on behalf of the temperance movement, which allowed the Wilson-Marshall ticket to win votes from some of the "bone-dry" contingent.

FRANKLIN D.

ROOSEVELT

★ 1933–1945 ★

"I THINK THIS WOULD BE A GOOD TIME FOR BEER."

—Franklin D. Roosevelt

AN END
TO PROHIBITION

CONSISTENTLY RANKED as one of America's greatest presidents, Franklin Delano Roosevelt deserves high marks for guiding the country through World War II and digging out from the Great Depression.

FDR's first presidential election victory in 1932 was partly the result of his belief that most voters were sick of Prohibition. A distant cousin of Teddy Roosevelt, Franklin—usually a man of moderation when he imbibed—often used drinking to break the ice in social situations. On those rare occasions when FDR did pass his typical two-cocktail limit, he held up well enough that even his enemies could not accuse him of drunkenness.

His daily drink rituals may have helped Roosevelt deal with some of the harsher realities of his life, such as his confinement to a wheelchair due to polio and his less-than-perfect marriage with the less-than-exciting Eleanor.

FDR enjoyed mixing gin-based martinis (and occasionally whiskey-based Manhattans) for guests as much as he liked drinking them, though his tendency to dump-and-stir won him no accolades as a bartender. He is most associated with cocktails, but enjoyed a variety of libations—including champagne, rum, brandy, and beer. He consistently drank in the White House, but sometimes upped his alcohol consumption when on a sailing trip or flicking the cards around a poker table. Details of such incidents are wonderfully chronicled in the diaries of Secretary of the Interior Harold L. Ickes.

FRANKLIN "SPIKE" ROOSEVELT

One of FDR's most outrageous stories (one he related in detail to Ickes during his first term) involved spiking a friend's drink—in his buddy's best interest, of course. The story, which dates back to FDR's pre–World War I days—and, frankly, sounds a bit embellished—goes like this:

Franklin knew a stockbroker down on his luck. After a few drinks with FDR, the hapless broker admitted that he was several thousand dollars in debt and saw no clear way out of his predicament. Later in the evening, Franklin, the broker, and a mutual friend wandered into a high-class New York City casino. The broker begged FDR and the third man to each lend him twenty-five dollars to gamble on a spinning wheel game—a desperate attempt to right the shipwreck of his personal finances.

Long story short, the broker was down to his last ten dollars when Lady Luck suddenly reversed course and planted a kiss upon his alcohol-flushed cheeks. He began to *win*: first five hundred dollars, and then a thousand, and then even more. That was the good news.

The bad news was that this "Wall Street Wally" also continued to drink and refused all pleas to leave with his winnings still intact. The boozy broker kept playing and risked losing it all back.

So what did his friends do? Franklin and his pal bought the already tipsy broker back-to-back drinks, spiked extra strong, and the broker finally cooperated by passing out. When the broker awoke in his hotel the next day, he had—along with a crushing hangover—all of his winnings and only a vague memory of how he'd secured the cash.

BEER FOR ALL

Most discussions about Franklin Delano Roosevelt and alcohol typically start with his desire to mix cocktails for his guests. That picture is accurate, but one plain sentence spoken to a national radio audience might be more significant.

"I think this would be a good time for beer," announced an upbeat FDR during one of his "fireside chats" in March 1933.

One can imagine the jubilation of the man on the street at such a simple sentence. After all, less than two years earlier, his presidential predecessor Herbert Hoover had been showered with boos and chants of "We want beer! We want beer!" while attending a World Series game in Philadelphia during Prohibition.

And now FDR was inviting them to *have* beer.

Roosevelt's stance on alcohol was founded in principle, not political convenience. He had always been tolerant of drinking, at least in moderate amounts. He had run, unsuccessfully, as the vice-presidential candidate with Jim Cox when the Republicans rode dark horse candidate Warren G. Harding to the White House in 1920. But Harding—a consistent drinker—hypocritically had no qualms about courting the support of the "dry" contingent.

All that said, FDR—running against the incumbent Herbert Hoover in 1932—knew the country was in need of a lift. The Great Depression was smothering the people, and he felt that moderate amounts of alcohol might help the masses to better cope with the daily struggle, as well as help stimulate the economy.

It would be a stretch to say that FDR won the White House chiefly by promising to roll back Prohibition. He believed the turning point of the election campaign came when Hoover sent the army in to clear out the tattered Bonus Army (thousands of World War I veterans who marched on Washington demanding cash-payment redemption of service certificates), using tear gas, horses, and tanks. The brutality of that action, deemed necessary by some, was splashed across the front pages of America's newspapers.

But the idea of bringing back beer did not hurt the Democratic cause, either. Days after Prohibition was repealed, the famous Budweiser beer wagon arrived in the capital. First marketed for this momentous occasion, the wagon's powerful Clydesdales clip-clopped down Pennsylvania Avenue with a gift of free brew for the new occupant of the White House. Yuengling—a Pottsville, Pennsylvania, operation that can trace its roots back to 1829—also

FDR'S RUM SWIZZLE

As a young man in 1921, FDR was diagnosed with crippling polio. His doctors had no hope of a cure to offer. Roosevelt, partly in an effort to remain upbeat and partly because he half-believed tropical climates might ease the effects of his disease, embarked on sailing trips in 1923 and 1924.

And rum was a standard part of those excursions.

Before one of his voyages, a friend sent Roosevelt an ensign (a signal flag or pennant) to display on the ship, and FDR joyfully fired off a thank-you letter proclaiming that he would hoist it to the mast and "salute it with 17 rum swizzles!"

Jean Edward Smith, author of the book *FDR*, not only records that exchange but—as if to participate in the fun—felt compelled to add a popular recipe (from FDR's time) for "Bermuda Rum Swizzles":

Bermuda Rum Swizzles

2 oz. dark rum

1 oz. lime juice

1 oz. orange juice

1 generous dash of Falernum (a sweet syrup)

Shake with ice. Strain into a highball glass filled with ice. Garnish with a slice of orange and a cherry.

> ## The President
> ## is quite fond of beer.

sent a truckload of specially brewed "Winner's Beer" to the White House for the occasion.

That FDR liked a few beers himself is a given. As a freshman at Harvard, young Franklin eagerly attended "beer night," a social icebreaker at the Ivy League institution. That taste for suds did not slacken over the years, as various entries in Ickes's diary attest. After the president returned from a Labor Day vacation on Vincent Astor's yacht, Ickes penned:

> September 5, 1933
> I have never seen [FDR] looking so well.... He said he had had three days of absolute rest where no one could get at him. He said that one night he had sat up until six o'clock in the morning playing poker and drinking beer and I remarked that if it had the effect on him that it appeared to have, he had better make a practice of it.

And several years later, Ickes hosted a poker game—one with both plenty of action and booze—and then noted:

> April 16, 1938
> ...we played poker until well after one o'clock. It was a lively game and the money changed hands pretty rapidly. I have had a bottle of 152-year-old Scotch whisky which I opened up for the occasion. I served this as a liquor after dinner as well as some 1811 Napoleon brandy. The President is quite fond of beer. He drank four bottles last night. The others preferred Scotch... I served Virgin Island rum cocktails before dinner and sparkling Burgundy during dinner.

Famed Broadway actress Helen Hayes Brown (a.k.a. "The First Lady of the American Theatre") could also attest to FDR's affinity for beer. Nervous to meet the president for the first time, she recalled a visit to the White House in her autobiography *My Life in Three Acts*:

> FDR was alone in the family sitting room. "I'm having a beer," he said. "What'll you have?" "The same," I answered. We sat chatting about this and that. All I remember is thinking that once I downed the beer I'd be free to disappear among the throng of foreign diplomats arriving downstairs.

When King George VI and Queen Elizabeth visited Hyde Park during their 1939 visit, much was made of the fact that hot dogs were served to the royals during a very informal picnic at the estate. FDR also offered the king and queen the perfect alcoholic beverage to accompany those hot dogs: American-brewed beer.

MIXOLOGIST-IN-CHIEF

Martha Gellhorn, a war correspondent and Ernest Hemingway's third wife, was sometimes invited to stay at the White House. Both President Roosevelt and his first lady Eleanor were fond of the globetrotting journalist.

But imagine Gellhorn's surprise when she found FDR mixing up a batch of martinis in the cloakroom, of all places, and giggling like a naughty schoolboy as he did it.

What could have driven FDR into the confines of the White House cloakroom? Most likely his mother's appearance for dinner and the knowledge that the Roosevelt matriarch not only disapproved of Franklin's imbibing, but also was quick to berate him for it.

Eleanor also disliked her husband's drinking habits. When FDR hosted his typical post-work, pre-dinner cocktail hour (he referred to it playfully as "the Children's Hour") straight-laced Eleanor was essentially banned—though she would occasionally attempt to disrupt the festivities under the pretense of bringing the president an important message.

But the main purpose of the Children's Hour was to unwind from work and chat about more frivolous topics. The cocktails assisted perfectly in that mission. The president loved to nudge his guests toward a refill with such playful lines as "How about another sippy?" or "How about a little dividend?"

Although he sometimes mixed up batches of Manhattans or Rum Swizzles, FDR was more noted for his gin martinis, with a little vermouth and a classic garnish of olives. Most people gave his martinis (barely) passing marks, but Hall Roosevelt (Eleanor's hard-drinking younger brother) dismissed FDR's concoctions as somewhat wimpy. Hall preferred more gin, less vermouth, and opted for what he considered a more masculine garnish—onions instead of olives.

WHEN BRANDY PROVED HANDY

FDR preferred cocktails on a daily basis, but he knew there were occasions that called for something more traditional, like brandy. One of those moments occurred during his 1940 presidential campaign against Republican Thomas Dewey. To combat the constant rumors of Roosevelt's ill health, FDR planned an open-car tour through several major cities. But when he got to New York City, the conditions deteriorated to a windy and bone-chilling rain. FDR toured through Gotham despite the weather but occasionally ducked into a garage for a change of dry clothes and—yes—a bracing glass of brandy to warm him up.

But FDR not only used brandy for medicinal purposes; he also summoned it when pondering a crucial decision.

In 1939, Roosevelt received a visit from Alexander Sachs, a prominent New York businessman. Wishing to persuade FDR to pursue research on building an atomic bomb, Sachs trotted out something of a cautionary tale: he mentioned that Napoleon had once been approached with the idea of constructing a fleet of combat-ready steamships, but Napoleon failed to explore this offer of new naval technology.

Perhaps the mention of the doomed French emperor was not lost upon FDR. He called for a well-aged bottle of Napoleon brandy (a bottle long in the Roosevelt family) and two glasses. Over the drinks, the men began to hash out a plan to beat Nazi Germany to the punch in acquiring what was to be, in that era, the world's most devastating weapon. One can almost smell the delectable fumes wafting up from the brandy snifters.

THE BRITISH ARE COMING!

During his three-plus terms as president, FDR had to entertain heads of state, generals, and diplomats from around the world. But three of the most important had to be the King and Queen of England, who came to visit both Washington and Hyde Park, New York, and Sir Winston Churchill, who visited Hyde Park and the White House on different occasions.

Roosevelt's mother, Sara, still felt she had the authority to control FDR's drinking. The president would often retreat to his study—off-limits to any would-be spoilsports—if he wanted a second drink without a garnish of criticism. A comical scene evolved from these differing opinions concerning alcohol when King George VI and Queen Elizabeth arrived at Hyde Park in 1939. As FDR's son James Roosevelt recalled in *My Parents*:

> Later granny served a formal dinner for the royal couple. To her horror, [FDR] had drinks brought out before dinner. He said to the King: "My mother thinks you should have a cup of tea. She doesn't approve of cocktails."
>
> The King, who had little to say, thought this over for a few minutes, then observed: "Neither does my mother." Whereupon they grabbed their glasses, raised them to one another in an unspoken toast and downed their martinis.

> Churchill was the best man that England had,
> even if he was drunk half of his time.

Prime Minister Churchill presented a different challenge. His demands for liquor when visiting the United States were legendary. A much-circulated story involved the bulldoggish PM explaining his various alcohol "must haves" to White House staffer Alonzo Fields: a tumbler of bedside sherry in the morning, a few glasses of scotch and soda before lunchtime, and French champagne and ninety-year-old brandy before he turned in after a long day.

Speaking of long days, it was said that Churchill's visits often required FDR to stay up well past midnight, something he rarely did on his regular schedule. Since most extended stints with Sir Winston typically involved more drinking, FDR sometimes needed extra rest and recovery once his esteemed visitor returned to England.

Whether he was completely serious or not, FDR's early-in-the-war assessment of the famous British leader (according to the Ickes diaries) was that Churchill was "the best man that England had, even if he was drunk half of his time."

At Hyde Park, James Roosevelt remembered Churchill quite vividly—pinky-pale, huddled beneath an umbrella by the pool—smoking a cigar and waiting for a full bottle of brandy to arrive. And, in something of an understatement, James Roosevelt added: "[Churchill] could do justice to a bottle of brandy."

LAST CALL

Once called upon to make a graduation day speech at West Point on a very sultry day, FDR was in need of something to keep his throat in working order. He opted for a libation that might have brought forth an enthusiastic "Bully for you!" from his relative Teddy Roosevelt—none other than the classic mint julep, a favorite of Teddy's.

HARRY S.

TRUMAN

★ 1945–1953 ★

"HUGO, I DON'T MUCH CARE FOR YOUR LAW,
BUT, BY GOLLY, THIS BOURBON IS GOOD."

—Harry S. Truman

"B"
FOR BOURBON

HARRY TRUMAN was not given a full middle name at birth—simply the letter "S." According to some accounts, "S" was arrived at because both of his grandfathers had an "S" that figured prominently in their names, and it was left at that so as not to favor one over the other.

Those interested in what presidents like to drink might have judged the letter "B" more appropriate given Truman's fondness for bourbon. What's particularly interesting is that the thirty-third president seemed to enjoy a shot of the amber-colored elixir not long after the break of dawn. But by no means did he limit his intake to that morning "nip."

The aftermath of Truman's attempt to seize control of the U.S. steel industry—a dubious move foiled by the Supreme Court—involved a peace offering of bourbon in its denouement. But with or without bourbon, Truman had plenty of truly tough decisions to make, including giving final approval to drop the atom bombs on Japan, as well as difficult choices during the Korean War, such as firing popular general Douglas MacArthur.

If there is a lasting image of Truman it is probably the one of him grinning as he holds up the *Chicago Tribune*—its front page erroneously proclaiming: "DEWEY DEFEATS TRUMAN." It certainly was an occasion to celebrate with a drink.

WEATHER, WHISKEY, AND DIAMONDS

Born in 1884 and raised near Independence, Missouri, young Harry Truman attempted to woo one of the town's best-known belles, Bess Wallace. He finally mustered up the courage to propose to her in a letter in 1911. Relying on such diverse topics as weather and whiskey before segueing into the true aim of his letter, Harry wrote:

> The elements evidently mistook one of my wishes for dry instead of wet. I guess we'll all have to go to drinking whiskey if it doesn't rain soon. Water and potatoes will soon be as much a luxury as pineapples and diamonds. Speaking of diamonds, would you wear a solitaire on your left hand should I get it?

Ms. Wallace managed to contain her enthusiasm for this initial proposal, but she did eventually marry Harry in 1919 after the then artillery captain returned from the battlefields of France.

THE FRENCH CONNECTION

Harry Truman had rarely been out of Missouri, but the Great War (as it did with many young American "doughboys") gave him a crash course in dealing with the French. Although a drink of whiskey was somewhat difficult to come by, the French soldiers and citizens had plenty of wine and brandy to offer, and the Americans were quite thirsty enough to accept.

Captain Truman commanded an artillery unit—Battery D, to be exact. On November 11, 1918, after days of rumors, the Germans signed an armistice and soldiers at the front received word to cease hostilities at 11:00 a.m. Truman's battery fired its last round about fifteen minutes before the war officially ended.

Then it got very quiet—but not for very long. As Truman later recalled:

> ...a great cheer rose all along the line. We could hear the men in the infantry a thousand meters in front

raising holy hell. The French battery behind our position were dancing, shouting and waving bottles of wine.... Celebration at the front went on the rest of the day and far into the night.

No doubt Truman would have preferred a shot of bourbon, but the occasion (and availability) called for French wine. And the jubilant French soldiers were more than willing to share.

I went to bed about 10 P.M. but the members of the French Battery insisted on marching around my cot and shaking hands. They'd shout "Vive le Capitaine Americain, vive le President Wilson," take another swig from their wine bottles and do it over. It was 2 A.M. before I could sleep at all.

Truman spent about a year in France, but he never became a fan of French wine—or, for that matter, French food. One of his handwritten letters to sweetheart Bess in January 1919 left no doubt of that, while reaffirming his appreciation of bourbon in the face of the recently enacted Prohibition. As Truman put it:

For my part I've had enough vin rouge and frog-eater victuals to last me a lifetime. And anyway it looks to me like the moonshine business is going to be pretty good in the land of Liberty loans and green trading stamps, and some of us want to get in on the ground floor. At least we want to get there in time to lay in a supply for future consumption. I think a quart of bourbon would last me about forty years.

THE BOYS FROM BATTERY D

Truman loved his men from Battery D and went out of his way to help organize and attend postwar reunions with those who served with him in France. The men loved Captain Truman, too, and more than one gave him credit for saving their lives.

THE MISSOURI MULE

Very few presidents can claim to have had a drink invented in their honor. Harry Truman, however, is among the chosen few. When President Truman would stay in London, he typically set up camp at the much-esteemed Savoy Hotel, which included the famed American Bar, featuring jazz and inventive U.S.-style cocktails.

A fixture for decades at the American was Belfast-born barman Joe Gilmore. Gilmore, who rose to head barman in 1955, created commemorative cocktails to honor famous people and historical occasions. To honor Truman, Gilmore created the "Missouri Mule." It was a clever name choice, given that Missouri (not to mention the Democratic Party) has long been associated with this hardworking animal. This drink—which suggests a mean "kick" if handled frivolously—requires bourbon as its main base, a few other liquors, and a vigorous shake or two.

Missouri Mule
2 parts bourbon whiskey
2 parts Applejack
1 part Campari
1 part Cointreau

Shake ingredients together with ice, and strain into a cocktail glass.

> I hope you fellows will stay sober at least until I'm inaugurated into office, then I don't care what you do.

The men admittedly were a rough and rowdy bunch, sometimes proving to be an embarrassment for Truman back in the States. For example, at one of the gatherings in the early 1920s, the boys of Battery D—obviously drunk (did Prohibition apply to war veterans?)—began tossing objects such as rolls, dinner plates, glasses, and even a sugar bowl at each other at an Elks Club they had rented out for the occasion. Although Truman was not one of the main combatants, it nevertheless fell on him to pay the damages the next day, which the future president sheepishly did.

By the time Truman ran for president in 1949, most of the surviving members of Battery D would have been over fifty. After he won, Truman invited them to a breakfast in the nation's capital, just prior to his inauguration. Remembering some of their past shenanigans, Truman felt compelled to issue a plea for good behavior. As Frederick Bowman, one of the former artillery men, recalled: "Well... he had a breakfast for the Battery and his parting words as we left... were, 'Well, I've got a very busy morning and I hope you fellows will stay sober at least until I'm inaugurated into office, then I don't care what you do.'"

TOASTING WITH "CACTUS JACK"

When Truman was sworn in as the new U.S. senator from Missouri in 1935, he was marched, along with other newcomers to Congress, before one of Washington's most famous political characters: John "Cactus Jack" Garner of Texas, who was then vice president. As witnessed by James Aylward, a Missouri political operator, who accompanied Truman to his swearing in:

> [Garner said] "Men, before we enter into these ceremonies, I'd like you all to join me in striking a blow

for liberty." So he got a jug that looked like corn liquor and we all pertook thereof.

Garner served as FDR's vice president (1933 to 1941), though it would be an understatement to say he found the job less than satisfying. In fact, Cactus Jack (who won this moniker because he once lobbied to have the prickly pear cactus named as the Texas "state flower") once infamously said that the vice president's position was "not worth a bucket of warm piss."

A SOBERING SUMMONS

Truman was quite content to be a senator. But in 1945, President Roosevelt tapped him to be his vice president (replacing Henry Wallace, who had succeeded Garner). Truman reluctantly agreed when FDR—peeved at Truman's initial resistance—played the "party loyalty" card.

Less than three months later, Truman adjourned the Senate and headed to House Speaker Sam Rayburn's office (a typical stop for Truman) for an end-of-the-day drink. But before Truman even had his bourbon, he was told to call Stephen Early, FDR's press secretary. Early told him to head to the White House immediately for an urgent announcement. By some accounts, Truman—sensing some sort of bombshell—blurted out: "Holy General Jackson!" and then hustled off to the White House.

When he got there, Truman was brought to Eleanor Roosevelt. The first lady gently informed him, "Harry, the President is dead." Briefly stunned, Truman naturally responded by asking Eleanor if there was anything he could do. Mrs. Roosevelt famously replied: "Is there anything we can do for you? Because you are the one in trouble now."

A MORNING WALK WITH OLD GRAND-DAD

President Truman's typical routine was to begin each day with a brisk walk, often as much as two miles, and afterwards he would enjoy a vigorous massage.

But it was what Truman did in between his morning walk and the massage that was really interesting: Truman knocked off an ounce or so of bourbon (typically Wild Turkey or Old Grand-Dad)—a classic "eye-opener" that the old artillery officer must have felt helped him take direct aim at the day.

STEEL, STRIKES, AND BOURBON

On April 8, 1952, President Truman attempted to take military control of the steel industry, fearing that a threatened national strike would hinder the American war efforts in Korea. Several months later, the Supreme Court ruled against the president. Truman was piqued that the court had defied him. Three days later, Supreme Court Justice Hugo Black invited the still-simmering president to an outdoor steak fry in a not-so-subtle attempt to smooth things over.

> We all went and poured a lot of bourbon down Harry Truman.... He didn't change his mind, but he felt better, at least for a few hours.

Bourbon was served, too. Truman sat almost silently for a while but eventually broke the tension with: "Hugo, I don't much care for your law, but, by golly, this bourbon is good."

In a 1972 CBS News interview, Justice William O. Douglas was a little more hard-boiled about Black's get-together, noting: "We all went and poured a lot of bourbon down Harry Truman.... He didn't change his mind, but he felt better, at least for a few hours."

TRAVELS WITH WINNIE

Truman and Winston Churchill respected and understood each other. Stunningly, Churchill failed in his reelection bid for prime minister in 1945. But when he arrived for an American visit in 1946, Truman was able to get Churchill to agree to a speaking engagement at tiny Westminster College in Fulton, Missouri. They headed west from Washington, D.C., but traveling with "Winnie" also meant meeting certain expectations. As General Harry Vaughan recalled:

> We got aboard the train and we'd gotten about...to Silver Spring [Maryland]. Mr. Churchill and his secretary...and the President and I were sitting there in the car. The President said: "What do you have to do to get a drink on this...thing?"
>
> So I pressed the button and a steward came in and pretty soon Mr. Churchill had a tall whiskey and soda in his hand. He held it up and let the light shine through it (it was about four o'clock in the afternoon) and he said: "You know, when I was a young subaltern in the South African War, the water was not fit to drink. To make it palatable, we had to put a bit of whiskey in it. By diligent effort I learned to like it."

When the party arrived in Fulton the next day, the Americans realized that they were in a "dry" town—a definite dilemma when one considered their distinguished guest and his well-known indulgences. At Truman's request, Vaughan rustled up a pint bottle of spirits somewhere.

> I went out to the kitchen and got some ice and a pitcher of water and a glass and went upstairs. Mr. Churchill was sitting there with his robe on and I said: "Mr. Churchill, here, I thought you might need a little pick-me-up before we go over to the gymnasium."
>
> "Well," he said. "General, am I glad to see you. I didn't know whether I was in Fulton, Missouri, or Fulton, Sahara."

Whatever libations Churchill consumed prior to his speech, it must have been precisely the right amount of fortification. Those in the audience were treated to one of Sir Winston's most famous postwar oratory efforts—"The Sinews of Peace"—far better known as his "Iron Curtain" speech.

THIRD TIME'S THE CHARM

After serving the Roosevelts for many years, White House butler-bartender Alonzo Fields considered himself a pro. But early in Truman's administration, first lady Bess asked for two pre-dinner cocktails—specifically, Old Fashioneds. Fields's first effort proved too weak for Bess's taste. So Fields, his pride slightly dented, dug up an alternative recipe. This attempt, too, fell short of the mark—apparently, a bit too fruity.

With a flash of frustration, Fields put two generous pours of bourbon over ice into bar glass tumblers and added a few bitters. This strong-on-the-bourbon, light-on-everything-else approach did the trick—and the president and the first lady complimented Fields on his creation.

THE TRUTH ACCORDING TO TRUMAN

On a visit to New York City, then former president Truman ducked into Bemelmans Bar at the Carlyle Hotel. Irish-born bartender Tommy Rowles was serving exactly his fourth customer of what was to be a fifty-plus-year career at that fine establishment. Nevertheless, he knew who Truman was.

"I'll tell you what he drank if you don't ask what time of day it was," Rowles joked with a *New York Times* writer in a 2012 article about the celebrated barman's retirement. Truman ordered an Old Grand-Dad on the rocks; no big surprise. But the former leader of the free world also asked Rowles if the young publican was allowed to join him.

"I told him I could drink, but I could never drink an Old Grand-Dad," remembered Rowles. Whereupon Truman asked the Irishman to look outside and report what he saw. A noisy gaggle of reporters and photographers, Rowles observed.

Then Truman smiled and said: "Yes, and if you had to walk fifteen blocks with these guys following you, you'd drink this, too."

LAST CALL

Truman enjoyed playing poker and sipping a few bourbons when he traveled on the presidential yacht.

A collector and seller of historical items recently featured a large sterling silver bourbon "jigger" (about two ounces) that was engraved with "HST" and the words "Only A Thimble Full." It was billed—like Harry himself—to be the real deal.

JOHN F.

KENNEDY

★ 1961–1963 ★

"I AM THE MAN WHO ACCOMPANIED
JACQUELINE KENNEDY TO PARIS,
AND I HAVE ENJOYED IT."

—John F. Kennedy

ALCOHOL
IN CAMELOT

MORE HAS BEEN WRITTEN about John Fitzgerald Kennedy than about any other American president—an estimated forty thousand books, just for starters. Some of this fascination no doubt arises from his tragic assassination on November 22, 1963.

Many Kennedy books wax eloquent in their worship of JFK and mourn the murdered president cut down near the pinnacle of his life. But other books that question and tarnish the Kennedy image and mystique also have emerged over the decades. For instance, Seymour Hersh's *The Dark Side of Camelot* alleges strong ties between patriarch Joe Kennedy and the Mafia, among other things.

Where does alcohol fit in when one talks about the Kennedys? Since it is virtually impossible to even run for president without truckloads of money to fund the effort, then one could speculate that JFK might not have ever entered the White House without the profits from alcohol, an early cornerstone of Joe Kennedy's multi-million-dollar empire.

On a more personal level, John Kennedy, the thirty-fifth president of the United States, liked alcohol, but he did not love or need it. Alcohol was more of a prop for his other interests—politics, recreation, male camaraderie, and female companionship. That said, it is hard to envision Camelot—or at least the Jack and Jackie version of it—without daiquiris, the occasional Bloody Mary, or the finest French champagne.

GOOD TIMES WITH JACK AND JACKIE

Arthur Schlesinger Jr. was an astute observer of the heady days of JFK. Schlesinger's journals (which he kept from 1952 to 2000) are an invaluable source for several presidents, but particularly JFK. Schlesinger served as an occasional speechwriter for JFK, and he sometimes spoke on behalf of the campaign. On June 12, 1960, Schlesinger wrote about his first trip to the Kennedy compound on Cape Cod: "We arrived about noon on a hot, overcast day. Jack and Jackie were playing croquet on the lawn with a couple of friends. They stopped and we had daiquiris on the terrace."

> Then we drank Bloody Marys, swam from the boat, and finally settled down for an excellent lunch.

And, similarly, on Aug 6 of the same year, Schlesinger arrived in Hyannis Port and joined Kennedy on a boating excursion: "Then we drank Bloody Marys, swam from the boat and finally settled down for an excellent lunch. After lunch, cigars and conversation...."

With JFK's political future on the rise, it all sounds pretty relaxing. But, then again, Kennedy wasn't yet in the Oval Office or facing off with Khrushchev over missiles in Cuba. That was all yet to come.

JFK'S TRUE INTOXICANT

Following JFK's inauguration ceremony, journalist Joseph Alsop remembered the new president's arrival at Alsop's Georgetown apartment a few hours after midnight—snow drifting down in flakes like heaven-sent confetti. The good host offered the new president a bowl of Maryland terrapin (a much-coveted dish in George Washington's era) and, of course, a glass of champagne.

He took the wine but needed no more than a glance to reject what had formerly been the greatest delicacy of the United States.

It hardly mattered. I soon observed that what he really wanted was one last cup of unadulterated admiration, and the people crowded around gave him that cup freely, filled to the brim.

NOT YOUR AVERAGE JOE

Kennedy patriarch Joseph Kennedy was worth millions, and much of that fortune was the result of shrewd setups he arranged on the eve of FDR's move to end Prohibition. Joe Kennedy (who also made money in other ways, including in banking, on Wall Street, and in the film industry) was appointed by FDR to be U.S. ambassador to England in 1933. Kennedy used some of his connections—including FDR's son, James Roosevelt—to line up contracts and warehousing for massive amounts of high-quality scotch and gin in Great Britain. When liquor was once again legal in the United States, few people were in a better position to capitalize on that change of events than Joe Kennedy.

It would be an understatement to say that not everybody was a Joe Kennedy fan. (As ambassador to England, for example, he predicted that Hitler and the Nazis would prevail over the British.) One non-fan was Harry Truman. Truman preferred bourbon and would always choose that drink over scotch whisky. Once asked why, Truman quipped something like: "You know, every time you drink a glass of scotch you put another quarter in Joe Kennedy's pocket!"

THE JFK BEER TAX

Although he had access to millions (and, as president, could direct billions with a stroke of a pen), some staffers in JFK's inner circle were perplexed to find that the president often had no money in his pocket. In fact, he sometimes would borrow ten dollars from White House staffers if he needed a haircut.

And there was never any change. JFK justified this by joking that it would even out the score for all the times his entourage had raided the president's beer supply.

A STAKE THROUGH THE "DRY" HEART

Although the Kennedy White House had sophisticated tastes—with French cuisine and French wine often front and center—advocates of temperance tried to make a "last stand" of sorts. They wanted at least to keep hard liquor banned from White House events. As the late journalist Helen Thomas wrote in her autobiography *Front Row at the White House*:

> It was held in the State Dining Room where open bars had been set up. In addition, butlers circulated through the rooms with trays of champagne and mixed drinks.
>
> The stories that appeared about the open bar unleashed a furor as certain parts of the country and one group in particular, the Women's Christian Temperance Union (WCTU) weighed in with their outrage. The first couple abandoned the practice, but later on it was quietly resumed, and during such functions, one could walk up to a strategically placed bar for a drink. It's hard to believe in this day and age that something like an open bar would prompt such a backlash—and the practice became White House routine over time.

One thing was apparent: The old-fashioned frumpiness of the Woman's Christian Temperance Union was no match for the youthful, dashing elegance of the Kennedy White House.

JFK SHAKES IT UP: THE CHAMPAGNE TWIST

The former *Washington Post* managing editor Ben Bradlee had a close-but-sometimes-awkward relationship with JFK. On one

> The champagne was flowing like the Potomac in flood, and the president himself was opening bottle after bottle...

hand, Bradlee and the president often attended the same dinners and cocktail parties; but JFK (despite the fact that the *Post* had endorsed him over Nixon) was nevertheless wary about what Bradlee printed or might print.

As far as JFK's drinking, Bradlee waited until 1975 when he published *Conversations with Kennedy* to mention much about it. Bradlee noted that he only saw JFK "tight" once, and that was after a very small dinner (sans Jackie, but with her younger socialite sister Lee Radziwill) at the White House.

> ...after dinner Lee Radziwill put Chubby Checker's records on and gave all the men lessons. The champagne was flowing like the Potomac in flood, and the president himself was opening bottle after bottle in a manner that sent the foam flying over the furniture, shouting "Look at Bill go" to Walton, or "Look at Benji go" to me, as we practiced with "the princess."

Bradlee, however, admitted that the "champagne twist" incident was an unusual "one off" for the president. More typically, JFK nursed a scotch and water, sipped his wine at dinner, and rarely indulged in a drink during the day.

FLYING HIGH ON AIR FORCE ONE

Since John Kennedy had an easygoing personality (particularly compared to his brother, Attorney General Robert Kennedy), it is not surprising that he allowed his White House staff to imbibe when traveling. The food on Air Force One even had a regional slant: New England clam chowder was often on hand.

JACKIE'S DAIQUIRIS

Jacqueline Kennedy's favorite drink was French champagne—and not just any champagne but Veuve Clicquot served in an elegant flute glass (something of a morbid irony, in hindsight, since this premium vintage from Reims is named for a nine-teenth-century French widow), However, Jackie also would occasionally kick back with a daiquiri. The Kennedys partic-ularly liked to serve daiquiris during summer get-togethers at their Cape Cod compound.

Here is a surprisingly simple recipe that Jackie Kennedy reportedly posted for her kitchen staffers to follow:

Jackie's Daiquiris
2 parts rum
2 parts frozen limeade
1 part fresh lime juice
dash of Falernum (a sweet syrup, 2 or 3 drops max, depending on how "tart" you want them)

Blend all the ingredients together and enjoy!

Drinks onboard included gin, scotch whisky, beer (JFK enjoyed Heinekens), wine, and the ever-present daiquiris. The president himself—true to form—rarely drank more than one or two. He did not chide others for drinking more, but sometimes just the hint of a disapproving look might bring an overly festive passenger to back off slightly. As noted in Kenneth T. Walsh's book *Air Force One*, Robert Kennedy also brought his rambunctious black Labrador onboard. One can picture the Lab causing a commotion by prancing around the cabin, whipping his tail about, and poking his nose wherever he pleased. The flight staff solved this problem by treating the canine to a martini, and he soon curled up for a nap.

Air Force One, of course, would become the backdrop for the terrible aftermath of JFK's assassination. With his casket onboard and Vice President Johnson waiting to be sworn in, aides of the slain president broke out the scotch whisky in a futile attempt to dull the shock and pain. But, as one of them said, even several glasses could not budge them from stone-cold soberness and the horrible reality—Jack Kennedy was dead.

It was hardly much better for those close to Kennedy who learned of it secondhand. As Schlesinger recorded in his November 23, 1963, journal entry:

> I heard the terrible news as I was sipping cocktails with Kay Graham, Ken Galbraith and the editors of *Newsweek*.... A man entered in his shirtsleeves and said, a little tentatively, "I think you should know that the President has been shot in the head in Texas." It took a few seconds for this to register. Then we all rushed for the radio.

LAST CALL

The Kennedy White House was a "happening" place, and countless celebrities were invited to dinners there

Schlesinger relates the funny story of the famed composer Igor Stravinsky, who was invited to a White House dinner held in his honor.

Schlesinger went over to talk to him, and Stravinsky implored him to lean closer so that he could whisper in Schlesinger's ear. "When I did," Schlesinger wrote, "he said, with a smile of great content on his face, 'I am drunk.'"

LYNDON B.

JOHNSON

★ 1963 – 1969 ★

"CONGRESS IS LIKE A WHISKEY DRINKER.
YOU CAN PUT AN AWFUL LOT OF WHISKEY INTO A MAN
IF YOU JUST LET HIM SIP IT. BUT IF YOU TRY TO FORCE
THE WHOLE BOTTLE DOWN HIS THROAT AT ONE TIME,
HE'LL THROW IT UP."

—Lyndon B. Johnson

A TALL
ORDER

LYNDON BAINES JOHNSON loyalists will point to the tall Texan's efforts (he stood at six feet three inches or so, second only to Honest Abe in presidential height) to advance civil rights and the enactment of the Great Society and the War on Poverty as his greatest achievements.

The Vietnam War, inherited from John F. Kennedy and expanded by the thirty-sixth president, led to LBJ's personal and political downfall and certainly played a major role in his decision not to seek a second term in 1968. "That bitch of a war..." was how he occasionally referred to it.

Regardless of his standing in history, it would be extremely difficult to defend LBJ's personal conduct. He could turn on the Texas charm when necessary, but it did not take much to flip his switch. As one newsman put it: "He'd call you in, give you whiskey, and joke with you. But he was a mean SOB, too."

Lyndon Baines Johnson, in fact, is arguably the crudest U.S. president in history, and probably by a wide margin. To take just one example, he had no qualms about urinating in front of others when nature called. That alcohol served as an accelerant to some of LBJ's gross and belligerent endeavors is without question.

DRINKIN' AND DRIVIN'

LBJ was long deceased when the British rock band The Business came out with the outrageously inappropriate tune "Drinking and Driving"—but he might have smiled at the title. Johnson apparently loved to drink and drive (at high speeds, too) and relished terrorizing anybody unsuspecting enough to jump into his Lincoln Continental and tour his "spread"—the president's sprawling Texas ranch near Stonewall.

Time magazine ran a story in April 1964 (titled "The Presidency: Mr. President, You're Fun") that documented one such episode, which LBJ biographer Robert Dalleck referred to as treating the Washington press corps to some "Texas-style drinking and driving." Johnson loaded four journalists into his Lincoln—under the usual pretense of touring the ranch—and soon had the Lincoln blasting away at full throttle. As the *Time* story told it:

> A cream-colored Lincoln Continental driven by the President of the United States flashed up a long Texas hill, swung into the left lane to pass two cars poking along under 85 miles per hour, and thundered on over the crest of the hill—squarely into the path of an oncoming car. The President charged on, his cup of Pearl beer within easy sipping distance. The other motorist veered off the paved surface to safety on the road's shoulder. Groaned a passenger in the President's car when the ride was over: "That's the closest John McCormack has come to the White House yet."

McCormack was speaker of the House and thus second in line for the presidency if LBJ had rolled his barreling Lincoln. The idea of a fatal crash did not seem entirely far-fetched. When Johnson finished his own beer, he helped himself to some of a female reporter's (Marinna Means, who gushed: "Mister President, you're fun!"—thus providing the title for the piece) and then took off at high speeds to go get more.

> The President charged on, his cup of
> Pearl beer within easy sipping distance.

At one point, one of the "lucky" press corps passengers along for this grand adventure glanced over at the speedometer and noticed that the needle was flirting with ninety miles per hour. LBJ responded by placing his cowboy hat over the speedometer so nobody could see how fast they were racing along the ranch roads.

Perhaps the riders in LBJ's Lincoln displayed needless apprehension: Johnson was an old hand at "drinkin' and drivin'," dating back to his pre-presidential days. According to Robert Caro—Johnson's most prolific biographer—LBJ drove a flashy yellow Buick in 1932, when he was a congressional secretary. According to Caro's *The Path to Power*, Johnson enjoyed driving people around in it, providing refreshment: "Loading them into the Buick, he drove them around, pulled out a bottle of whiskey, bragging about famous people that he knew."

Another trick LBJ sometimes enjoyed in his later years was driving unsuspecting passengers right into a lake on his ranch. As the vehicle careened downhill toward the body of water, LBJ would bellow that the brakes weren't working, terrifying the passengers. But Johnson secretly knew that the car was in fact a specialized amphibious vehicle.

STEP IT UP

Being on LBJ's Secret Service detail was no easy task and required at least one duty that the agents had not previously trained for: "running bartender."

When Johnson would tour his ranch, he would sometimes drive his Lincoln while the agents charged with his protection trailed a little bit behind in a station wagon. Since LBJ occasionally enjoyed a scotch or two on these tours—and would sometimes require a refill—it was the additional duty of the Secret Service men to see that he got it.

LBJ would cut off the agents by stopping his Lincoln, putting his arm out the window, and rattling the diminishing ice cubes in his plastic foam cup. An agent would then scurry up from the trail car, trot back to the car, make the president another scotch, soda, and ice, then hasten it back to the thirsty commander in chief.

THE THREE-SAM SLAM

Three men named Sam played key roles in Lyndon Johnson's life—and all three were well acquainted with alcohol.

Lyndon's father, Sam Ealy Johnson Jr., was a colorful politician from the Texas Hill Country (a large expanse of land rolling west of Austin). He bucked the forces of Prohibition in the 1920s—a stance that was as popular as beer and pretzels with the German-American and Czech-American constituents in his district. But Sam Johnson failed to make any lasting mark in the political ring. He also lost the family farm after cotton prices tumbled in the early 1920s. That experience seems to have left LBJ with some lasting empathy for the poor and disenfranchised.

A second "Sam"—Sam Rayburn—also helped guide Lyndon's career. Rayburn was famous for his "Board of Education" room at the Capitol where members of Congress (even some opposition Republicans) gathered for a drink or two after a long day at the political grindstone. Rayburn, the speaker of the House, allegedly pressured a freshman congressman to vote along with the Democrats. The political newbie squirmed and mumbled something about not wishing to disappoint his major contributors, who wanted him to vote the other way. "Son," Rayburn supposedly pontificated, "if you can't take their money, drink their whiskey, screw their women, and then vote against 'em, you don't deserve to be here."

Rayburn did not immediately admit LBJ into his sanctuary—despite the fact he was a fellow Texan. But once he did, the two men became close, almost like father and son, according to various Johnson aides.

The third "Sam" was Sam Houston Johnson—LBJ's younger brother. It may have been a jinxed name choice from the get-go, since the original Sam Houston—the hero of the Battle of San Jacinto and the first president of the Republic of Texas—brawled with John Barleycorn for much of his life. (The Cherokees sometimes called Houston "Big Drunk," referring to both his size and the amount of alcohol he could consume.)

Sam Houston Johnson also had alcohol problems, which sabotaged his fragile relationship with Lyndon and his wife, Lady Bird. When LBJ was a fast-rising congressman, Sam would crash at their Washington, D.C., apartment. Both Lady Bird Johnson and SHJ himself (in his book *My Brother Lyndon*) documented an uncomfortable incident involving the two men. LBJ apparently drank too much at a rain-soaked golf outing and arrived home soaked (in all meanings of that word) to find Sam once again asleep on his couch. As Jan J. Russell noted in her biography *Lady Bird*:

> Lady Bird woke up to the sound of Lyndon yelling at his brother. "I want Sam Houston to look at me," he told her. "Yes, by God, I want you to take a damned good look at me. I'm drunk, and I want you to see how you look to me, Sam Houston, when you come home drunk."

Although she was far from a Sam Houston fan, Lady Bird eventually had to step in and calm down her irate husband.

ALCOHOL AS A VOTING LUBRICANT

Like George Washington, Andrew Jackson, and William Henry Harrison—to name just a few—Johnson had no qualms about dispensing alcohol on the campaign trail. While running for Congress in 1937, Johnson rolled out the beer barrels to quench the thirst of potential voters, particularly in some

A TRUE TEXAN

The first U.S. president born in Texas is Dwight D. Eisenhower. But he moved to Kansas at the tender age of two, and considered that his home. So that makes LBJ the first "true" Texan in the White House. And the most truly Texan cocktail is the margarita. Forget pre-made mixes and blenders—this is the real deal. It may not be as sweet as what many are used to, but it's all Texas.

The True Texas Margarita
1½ oz. blanco (silver) tequila
1 oz. fresh lime juice
½ oz. triple sec

Moisten the rim of a cocktail glass with a lime wedge and dip into a small plate of salt to coat the rim. Chill the glass. Pour the ingredients into a shaker half full of ice cubes and shake vigorously. Strain into the glass.

counties of his district where there were many voters of German and Czech ancestry.

While young George Washington paid a rather hefty sum for the alcohol he supplied to voters in his House of Burgesses election, Johnson went the father of our country one better. According to Randall Woods (author of *LBJ: Architect of American Ambition*), the wily Texan somehow got Anheuser-Busch to provide free beer for his campaign. Anheuser-Busch (the company that makes Budweiser) already had a solid connection to the Democratic Party; the brewers sent Franklin Delano Roosevelt some free Bud for his role in repealing Prohibition.

JOHNSON IN CONTROL

Johnson was famous for drinking the soft drink Fresca in the White House during working hours, but he did not hesitate to bring out the hard stuff (typically, Cutty Sark scotch for himself) when he was attempting to rally support for a bill he wanted passed. LBJ sometimes walked around with a scotch and soda in his hand, but his staff was under strict orders to keep his on the weak side. Not so with other guests, and it did not take long for the president to work this to his political advantage.

A prime example was presented in Joseph Califano Jr.'s book *The Triumph and Tragedy of Lyndon Johnson*. The author (special assistant to Johnson starting in 1965) revealed that LBJ might have a very weak scotch, while Republican Senator Everett Dirksen would be treated to his favorite—Jack Daniel's bourbon—but with perhaps three times as much whiskey. A visitor, then, might be under the false assumption that he was matching LBJ drink for drink but was, in fact, consuming three times as much as his bigger—and craftier—host.

DR. LBJ: BOOZE, BEEFSTEAK, AND BABES

Everett Dirksen was a powerful Republican senator from Illinois, but Johnson—both as a fellow congressman and later as president—sometimes teamed up with him for bipartisan causes.

For example, LBJ was able to convince Dirksen that he should support civil rights legislation, reminding Dirksen that the senator was from the Great Emancipator's home state. Not surprisingly, some of these deals and compromises were hashed out over a bottle of bourbon or scotch.

When Dirksen (who supposedly once quipped that "champagne was his vegetable") was hospitalized with a bleeding ulcer in February 1964, LBJ was quick to phone in some humorous support and some Texas-styled medical advice. Thanks to taped White House telephone conversations (released in the 1990s), we know the conversation flowed exactly like this:

> LBJ: How're you feelin'?
> Dirksen: Well, I'm doing pretty good. That ulcer hit me last night about midnight.
> LBJ: You quit drinking that damned Sanka and get on a good Scotch whiskey [sic] once in a while!
> Dirksen: You got a point there.
> LBJ: ...What you need to do is go out and get you about three half glasses of Bourbon whiskey. Then go down to the Occidental [a Washington, D.C., restaurant] and buy a red beefsteak, and then get you a woman. So maybe that's what you need. Instead of drinking Sanka.
> Dirksen: (chuckles) You've got an idea.

THE JOHNSON TREATMENT

Avid readers of LBJ biographies or articles have probably encountered the phrase "The Johnson Treatment." For those unacquainted with the term, the Johnson Treatment occurred when LBJ approached someone, got disconcertingly close to his face (regardless of lunch, cigarettes, scotch, or whatever else might have been lingering on LBJ's breath), and then "persuaded" him to his own way of thinking, profanely if necessary. As Hubert Humphrey noted in his oral history for the LBJ Presidential Library:

Johnson got votes by whispering in ears and pulling
lapels, and nose to nose.... He'd just lean right in on
you, you know.... He was so big and tall he'd be kind
of looking down on you... pulling on your lapels and
he'd be grabbing you.... Even if he wasn't asking you
to vote for something, he'd be talking about the bill
in such a way that you knew what he had in mind.

Keep in mind that Humphrey (who became LBJ's vice-presidential candidate in 1964) was almost always on Johnson's side.
One can only imagine the full brunt of the Johnson Treatment
concentrated upon a perceived enemy.

WOULD YOU LAHK TA DANCE?

The Johnson Treatment became even weirder when LBJ had
knocked down a few drinks. Journalist Robert Novak was once
treated to just such a strange spectacle. Back in early 1960, when
Johnson was still a U.S. senator, Novak and fellow journalist Bob
Jensen of the *Buffalo Evening News* were enjoying a drink at the
National Press Club bar. The men were "off duty," but their R&R
was soon interrupted when someone barged into the bar and
announced that Lyndon Johnson was in the adjacent ballroom
and apparently "drunk as a loon."

The lure of this possibility was too much, and Novak hustled next
door, where he found LBJ exuberantly intoxicated. As Novak
related in his book *The Prince of Darkness*:

The report was not exaggerated. Johnson was attending the 70th birthday party of Bascom Timmons, a
famous Texas journalist who headed his own Washington news bureau. To my surprise, I found the
majority leader without aides or limo. LBJ, who until
then had shown little interest in me and absolutely no
affection, spotted me and wrapped one of his long
arms around me. "Bob, I like ("lahk" was the Texas

> Lyndon Johnson was in the adjacent ballroom and apparently "drunk as a loon."

pronunciation) you," he drawled drunkenly, "but you don't like me." He chanted it over and over, embracing me and swirling me in a little dance.

Novak observed that the rest of the revelers at the party seemed equally incapacitated. So the journalists felt compelled to assist LBJ, and—not without effort or charity—they guided the big Texan down to the street and dumped him into a homeward-bound taxi.

Did the future president thank Novak the next time he saw him? He did not. But he did mention the incident.

Novak was among reporters who approached "a cool immaculately groomed" Senator Johnson the next day, hoping to get a few minutes of Q&A before the Senate convened. Johnson looked up, perhaps feigning surprise at the reporters around him, but quickly singled out Novak and, as the journalist later wrote, said:

> "Well, Novak, saw you at the Press Club last night. Got a little drunk out, didn't it?"
>
> The other reporters chuckled appreciatively, thinking it was I who had been "a little drunk," as LBJ intended.

LAST CALL

LBJ had surprising success with getting most of his favorite legislation through Congress. The key, according to LBJ, was to gradually introduce bills. He once explained it like this to Joseph Califano: "Congress is like a whiskey drinker. You can put an awful lot of whiskey into a man if you just let him sip it. But if you try to force the whole bottle down his throat at one time, he'll throw it up."

CARTER

★ 1977–1981 ★

"WE ARE OVER-LAWYERED
AND UNDER-REPRESENTED."
—James Carter

THE
GEORGIA BOY

JAMES EARL "JIMMY" CARTER—a graduate of the U.S. Naval Academy and a Democratic governor of Georgia—typically gets low marks as a president.

But whatever Carter's shortcomings, it is safe to say that they cannot be blamed on his own consumption of alcohol, since he rarely imbibed, and then only very sparingly.

In fact, Carter, the thirty-ninth president, famously made war on the "three-martini lunch" and stopped serving hard alcohol at the White House. This is in spite of the fact that Carter, like most presidents, certainly had reason to hoist a few.

Carter's brother Billy, however, drank enough for the two of them—and then some. Billy's various shenanigans—most of which were doubtless in part influenced by alcohol—proved embarrassing to his presidential older brother. This included the awkward fad of "Billy Beer," an alcohol flop brewed by Falls City Brewing Company. But Billy was not completely alone; others from Carter's "inner circle" caused him alcohol-related problems, too.

Moreove, Carter's wife Rosalynn preferred to leave hard liquor off the menu at White House events. His mother Lillian, on the other hand, was more free-spirited and loved to knock back a bourbon or two.

WAR ON THE MARTINI LUNCH

Jimmy Carter became unpopular in his one term for lots of reasons—such as the boycott of the Moscow Olympic Games, long gas lines, the Iranian hostage crisis, and, yes, his war on the "three-martini lunch." Carter felt that hotshot business executives should not be allowed to write off pricey, booze-blasted lunches on their expense accounts while the working class guys could not do the same for their bologna sandwiches or street vendor hot dogs.

An unexpected side effect of Carter's attack on the three-martini lunch was that it moved both Gerald Ford and Barry Goldwater to respond with humorous declarations—something neither of these Republican stalwarts were typically inclined to do. Ford, who enjoyed martinis, said: "The three-martini lunch is the epitome of American efficiency. Where else can you get an earful, a bellyful, and a snootful at the same time?"

Not to be overshadowed, Goldwater (who often unabashedly broke out a bottle of Old Crow bourbon in his Senate office at the end a hard day) quipped: "None of us had a three-martini lunch until Carter was elected."

CRAFT BREWERS ROCK

Lest one think that President Carter's attack on martinis proves he was an ultra-religious spoilsport, it warrants noting that in 1979 he deregulated the American beer industry. It was the first time since Prohibition that it was once again legal to sell hops, malt, and brewer's yeast to homebrew aficionados in the States. So, if you recently cooked up a batch of home brew and are lifting a mug of fresh India pale ale to your lips, take time to toast James Earl Carter.

ROSALYNN'S RULES

The Carter White House years were far from a freewheeling time for diplomats or press corps members who liked to drink the hard stuff. Official dinners or receptions were not exactly a throwback to the days of teetotalers, but the situation and general vibe would have caused some consternation for whiskey or vodka drinkers or even those inclined to look for rapid refills.

The prim and proper Rosalynn Carter (her mother once said she was the kind of girl who could put on a white dress and keep it clean all day) admittedly had a dislike for hard alcohol—to the point that she found the mere appearance of it to be distasteful. As the former first lady once stated to a *Vanity Fair* writer:

> We served wine, punch, and cordials. That was what was served at the White House before John Kennedy. I had been to one dinner at the Nixon White House, when Jimmy was governor. It was so beautiful and so elegant and I was so impressed. Then here comes a waiter carrying a tray with bottles of liquor on it. I just did not like that. Everybody thought it was because we were Baptists, but it was not. I just thought it distracted from the elegance of the evening. And Jimmy agreed.

BILLY BEER

It is safe to assume that "Billy Beer" was not on Rosalynn's list of drinks considered classy enough to be served in the White House. It is also possible that she would have considered Billy Carter not classy enough to be allowed in the White House, either. In fact, Billy—the president's younger brother—was a stark reminder of that old phrase: "You can choose your friends, but not your relatives."

> Yes, I'm a real southern boy. I got a red neck, white socks, and Blue Ribbon beer.
>
> —Billy Carter

ONLY ON OCCASION

The Carters were not big drinkers. Well, Billy was, but Jimmy and Rosalynn were quite temperate. Or at least that was the conventional wisdom. But according to Ronald Kessler, the president was observed to have enjoyed a martini on occasion. For Jimmy's Georgian heritage, we offer the Georgia Martini.

The Georgia Martini

2 oz. peach vodka
½ oz. triple sec
1 oz. cranberry juice
1 oz. fresh lime juice

Pour all ingredients into a shaker half full of ice. Shake vigorously and strain into a chilled cocktail glass.

Once Jimmy Carter was in the national spotlight, it did not take very long for the press to figure out that Billy—a gas-pumping, beer-guzzling good ol' boy from Plains, Georgia—could create some copy on a slow news day. Billy once proudly told reporters: "Yes, I'm a real southern boy. I got a red neck, white socks, and Blue Ribbon beer."

But Billy's quips and hee-haw mannerisms took him beyond Blue Ribbon beer—he promoted his own brew called "Billy Beer." The first batches were brewed in July 1977 by the Falls City Brewing Company. The cans were labeled with a quote attributed to Billy: "I had this beer brewed up just for me. I think it's the best I've ever tasted. And I've tasted a lot. I think you'll like it, too."

The beer turned out to be a fad, then a complete flop; it is almost impossible to find anyone who will claim it tasted good. By 1978 (according to the *New York Times*), Reynolds Metals purchased close to nine million empty "Billy" cans (ones that never had beer in them, not ones emptied by thirsty aficionados of hops and malted beverages) and melted them down. But you can still buy a can of Billy Beer (a full one or an empty) on eBay or similar sites.

Just months after Reynolds melted down the Billy Beer cans, Billy himself had something of a meltdown. In March 1979 the president's brother—who sometimes drank beer for breakfast—entered the Long Beach Naval Hospital in California in an effort to "dry out." There is strong evidence that Billy never had another drink after he left rehab. Jimmy Carter has been quoted as saying: "The only one of our family who really suffered because of [my presidency] was my brother Billy."

A "ROAD-IE" WITH MISS LILLIAN

Carter's mother, Lillian Carter (a.k.a. Miss Lillian), occasionally liked to drink bourbon. In Robert Scheer's book *Playing President: My Close Encounters with Nixon, Carter, Bush I, Reagan, and Clinton—and How They Did Not Prepare Me for George W. Bush*, he writes that he was

> Gloria had carefully prepared two jars of liquid refreshment—one filled with Early Times bourbon and the other with water.

invited to a fish fry in Plains, Georgia, where Jimmy Carter "looked about as relaxed as one of the flapping fish in the drained pond." Scheer found Miss Lillian and Carter's sister Gloria much more fun:

> But Carter does come from a delightfully informal family. On one earlier occasion, Gloria and Miss Lillian had invited me to go along for supper at a local diner. Gloria had carefully prepared two jars of liquid refreshment—one filled with Early Times bourbon and the other with water—so I "wouldn't get thirsty" on the way to the dinner. While we were there, they playfully felt under my coat to see if I was wired for sound and became totally relaxed as they sipped on the bourbon and talked irreverently about the foibles of people in Plains.

Miss Lillian was once quoted to the tune of: "I know folks all have a tizzy about it, but I like a little bourbon.... It helps me sleep. I don't care much what they say about it."

Apparently, one guy who saw things Miss Lillian's way was Hubert Humphrey. In the late 1960s, Humphrey (then vice president under LBJ) visited Georgia and met a young Jimmy Carter, who was not yet in the political game. Humphrey learned that Miss Lillian was then working in the Peace Corps in a rather remote village in India. Through his Peace Corps connections, the vice president saw to it that Miss Lillian received a fifth of better-than-your-average bourbon.

THE RUSSIAN FACTOR

In 1979, Jimmy Carter met with Soviet president Leonid Brezhnev at the American Embassy in Vienna, Austria, for talks on limiting the deployment of nuclear weapons. As was typical with Russian leaders and diplomats, some drinking of toasts inevitably came into play. Needless to say, this was not Carter's strong suit. In his book *Keeping the Faith: Memoirs of a President*, Jimmy Carter admits Brezhnev sensed his weakness in this particular arena.

> We served them (the Russians) a drink, and Brezhnev immediately asked for supper. He was only half joking. Brezhnev and I discussed wine, grandchildren, the shortage of gasoline in both countries.... The meal was served as soon as it was ready, because Brezhnev clearly wanted to retire early. During supper we offered several toasts, and he bottomed up his glass of vodka each time, teasing me when I failed to do the same.

At a follow-up meeting at the Soviet Embassy, the peanut farmer from Plains figured out how to keep up with Brezhnev—without suffering great consequences during the event or, for that matter, the next day.

> Again Brezhnev offered frequent toasts. I arranged with the waiter for a tiny glass, shifted to a somewhat milder drink, and joined in the "bottoms up" ceremonies along with everyone else. There was a lot of jovial banter....

Always playing his cards tight to the vest, Carter does not tell us exactly what this "milder drink" was. White wine? Perrier? Georgia's own Coca Cola? We just don't know.

LAST CALL

According to the Secret Service agents in Ronald Kessler's book *In the President's Secret Service: Behind the Scenes with Agents in the Line of Fire and the Presidents They Protect*, the Carters asked for (and got) Bloody Marys before attending church on their first Sunday in the White House. One agent claimed that—contrary to their teetotaler reputations—Jimmy would occasionally have a martini or a light beer, and Rosalynn would have a very occasional screwdriver. The agents also reported that Miss Lillian once appeared at the White House door with two six-packs of beer in a paper bag intended for them. They appreciated the gesture but allegedly declined the gift.

Jimmy Carter's healthy lifestyle—including his very moderate imbibing of alcohol—must be viewed as a successful formula for longevity. As of this writing (October 2023), Carter is nintey-nine years old—almost six years older than his former rival for the longest-lived president, Gerald Ford.

WILLIAM J.

CLINTON

★ 1993–2001 ★

"I'M RELIEVED THAT I NEVER HAD A CRAVING
FOR [LIQUOR]. I HAVE ENOUGH PROBLEMS WITHOUT
THAT ONE."

—William J. Clinton

A MEET-AND-GREET WITH DESTINY

AS A TEENAGER, Bill Clinton traveled to Washington, D.C., with a student group from his home state of Arkansas. The main event was a meet-and-greet at the White House Rose Garden, where young Clinton shook hands with then president John Fitzgerald Kennedy.

It is not a stretch to suggest that that handshake helped illuminate the political path for Clinton. Imagine crossing a swiftly moving river, hopping from one inviting stone to another. That's sort of what Clinton did—he hopped from Georgetown University to Oxford as a Rhodes Scholar, to Yale Law School, to governor of Arkansas, and, eventually, in 1992, into the White House.

Not that there weren't occasional slipups during his otherwise successful term as the forty-second president. Clinton was accused of numerous extramarital affairs; then there were the "Whitewater" scandal and a messy impeachment for perjury and obstruction of justice.

But Clinton—with great oratory skills, a top-rate intellect, and some luck—survived it all.

Whatever Bill Clinton's personal flaws, drinking to excess is never mentioned among them. As he wrote in his autobiography: "A few times in my twenties and early thirties I might have had too much to drink.... But fortunately, liquor never did that much for me.... I'm relieved that I never had a craving for it. I have enough problems without that one."

ROUGH START

Bill Clinton's biological father—William Jefferson Blythe—died in a car crash three months before Bill was even born. His mother, Virginia, remarried, and the future president grew up with Roger Clinton as his stepfather.

One explanation for Clinton's go-easy attitude when it comes to drinking is that Roger Clinton was an alcoholic, with violent tendencies when he drank too much. As Clinton recalled in his autobiography *My Life*:

> One night his [Roger Clinton's] drunken self-destructiveness came to a head in a fight with my mother I can't ever forget…. They were screaming at each other in their bedroom in the back of the house. For some reason, I walked out into the hall to the doorway of the bedroom. Just as I did, Daddy pulled a gun from behind his back and fired in Mother's direction….

Young Clinton and his mother literally dodged a bullet, fled to a neighbor's house, and called the police. Clinton's stepfather was carted off in handcuffs in front of young Bill and his mother.

Roger Clinton did come back and stayed sober for some time, but his relapses eventually drove Clinton's mother to flee with her boys (Bill and younger half-brother, little Roger) and file for divorce. President Clinton and his stepfather reconciled later in their lives. Bill learned from his stepfather's struggles. "I hated what liquor had done to Roger Clinton" Clinton once wrote, "and I was afraid that it might have the same effect on me."

MY THREE BUDS

The antics of staff or family members might drive a president to drink, but the reverse can sometimes be true as well. Dealing with the drama in Bill Clinton's political career, for example, certainly tested the mettle of his staffers.

> I will never forget how good that beer tasted. Then I went back to being a political professional.

Clinton was building political momentum prior to the 1992 presidential election when the Gennifer Flowers allegations broke (she claimed Clinton had carried on a twelve-year affair with her). In something of a gamble, Clinton agreed to a *60 Minutes* interview in late January—knowing full well that he would be grilled on the latest accusations.

Somehow candidate Clinton (with wife Hillary Rodham Clinton by his side) managed to escape with limited damage (and without giving a "yes" answer in regards to Flowers's charges). He went on to gain the Democratic nomination that summer and then defeat President George H. W. Bush in November.

James Carville, Clinton's chief strategist, was perhaps as nervous as the governor and Mrs. Clinton through the grueling ordeal of the *60 Minutes* interview. As Carville relates in an insightful book called *All's Fair: Love, War and Running for President*:

> I had said, "Man, whatever you do, tell them to put about three cold Budweisers on ice." And when we got to the governor's suite I chug-a-lugged them. I know it sounds ridiculous, but that damn ordinary mass-produced Budweiser tasted better than the best glass of Chateau Margaux anybody ever had. I will never forget how good that beer tasted.
>
> Then I went back to being a political professional.

One can only speculate that Governor Clinton and Hillary may have indulged in a drink or two after the *60 Minutes* interview was over, too.

SNAKEBITE WILLIE

When former president Clinton arrived in Great Britain for the Yorkshire International Business Convention in 2001, he eventually found himself in a Harrogate establishment called the Old Bell Pub. A widely circulated story claims that Clinton requested a Snakebite—a half hard cider, half beer drink that he remembered trying from his student days at Oxford.

The publican turned down his request, claiming that they were not allowed to serve that particular drink. To which Clinton was said to have replied: "Well, that's too bad then, because you won't get to see my true personality." The Old Bell Tavern landlord Jamie Allen has been quoted in the British press about Clinton's request and Allen's refusal.

The pub's special guest then sampled a few kinds of British ale, but, according to some accounts, settled on a Coke to go with his steak and ale pie.

The Snakebite (a.k.a. Bill Clinton's Lament)
Hard cider
Lager beer

Pour 8 oz. of hard cider into a chilled glass. Float 8 oz. of chilled lager beer on top of the hard cider. (Pour over the back of a spoon to do this delicately.)

(Add a ¼ oz. of black currant liqueur for a Snakebite variation the Brits call "Diesel.")

PHOTO OPS

Although Bill Clinton was a very moderate drinker, a quick Internet search can produce some pictures of him toasting with a variety of world leaders. Like Reagan before him and Obama after him, President Clinton certainly understood the value of the "drinking photo op." Of course, some photo ops are more noteworthy than others. For example, former president Clinton met with Peru's Alan Garcia in 2009 as part of the Clinton Global Initiative program, and there is a photo of them drinking a Pisco Sour toast. (A Pisco Sour is made from Pisco, a powerful grape brandy native to Peru and Chile.)

In 1994, Bill Clinton traveled to Prague to meet with Czech president Vaclav Havel, and the former playwright knew just where to take his American visitor in the historic city. Havel took Clinton to a wood-paneled, working-class drinking spot called U Zlateho Tygra ("The Golden Tiger") and knocked back a few pints of the authentic Czech pilsner. One story has it that Clinton enjoyed three pints at the Golden Tiger and then opted to skip his daily jog the next morning.

On the same trip, Havel took Clinton to Prague's prestigious Reduta Jazz Club, where the president was presented with a Czech saxophone. Clinton (who had a lifelong interest in music and once played his sax on the Arsenio Hall Show) responded by playing a few tunes, including Elvis Presley's "Heartbreak Hotel"—Elvis being one of his late mother's favorite artists.

The Prague excursion was one of Clinton's most memorable. When Havel died, the president reminisced about the days he spent there in 1994 and about the famous Czech who sacrificed so much of his life to bring democracy to his country. He was, Clinton emphasized, "a big personality." Coming from the gregarious Bill Clinton—a man who scores large on the "likeability" scale—that's quite a compliment.

I SAW THE SIGN

At least two pubs in the United Kingdom have signs claiming that Bill Clinton once visited. At the Old Bell Pub in Harrogate, Yorkshire—scene of the alleged Snakebite request—a sign claims:

> This plaque commemorates the visit to Old Bell Tavern on Friday, 8th June 2001 of William Jefferson Clinton sometimes President of the United States of America, charismatic leader of the free world and (alleged) philander [sic]. He sat adjacent to this spot and enjoyed an Old Bell Steak & Ale pie!

An even more "cheeky" sign has been displayed at the Turf Tavern, an establishment that claims (among other things) to date back to the thirteenth century. The sign reads:

> IT IS ALLEGED THAT IT WAS HERE AT THE TURF TAVERN THAT BILL CLINTON WHILE AT UNIVERSITY HERE IN OXFORD, DURING THE SIXTIES "DID NOT INHALE" WHILST SMOKING AN ILLEGAL SUBSTANCE

And then, in a thinly veiled reference to the Lewinsky episode, the sign adds:

> (WHAT HE DOES WITH CIGARS IN HIS OWN HOME IS HIS BUSINESS)

"Slick Willie" and his bodyguards left the pub without paying—the lingering tab just over thirty-six dollars.

BILL BOLTS BILL?

What is it with Bill Clinton and British pubs? In December 2000, President Clinton, while accompanying Hillary and daughter Chelsea on a London shopping trip, opted for the classic male "I-think-I-need-a-beer" detour. (The Clinton women kept shopping.) The Secret Service checked out the place in advance, and so Clinton sauntered into the Portobello Gold Pub in Notting Hill. He grabbed a quick lunch and chased it down with a half-pint of Pittsfield's organic lager.

What happened next is, as the Brits might put it, a bit "dodgy." Simply stated, "Slick Willie" and his bodyguards left the pub without paying—the lingering tab just over thirty-six dollars.

Pub proprietor Michael Bell was quick to say that he did not believe that the president purposely did what the Brits are fond of calling "a runner" (i.e., eat, drink, don't pay, take off with preplanned haste); he was fairly certain that Clinton simply forgot.

When word leaked out about the incident, the British tabloid the *Mirror* could not help giving President Clinton "the business." They slapped "We Pay Bill's Bill" on page one after paying the president's tab for him; but then the U.S. Embassy felt obligated to cough up the sum to the tabloid.

Publican Michael Bell ran with the joke and claimed he also received reimbursement from "Socks"—"Socks" being the Clinton family cat. Bell told a British newspaper that a note came with the fee, and it read: "Please forgive me. I thought I trained my human better but every now and again I catch him going on the carpet. Hope this settles the tab."

BORIS GETS HIS PIZZA

FDR and Truman may have had their hands full when Sir Winston Churchill came to visit, but Bill Clinton had to deal with Russian president Boris Yeltsin. Even by Russian standards, Yeltsin was a notorious drinker, but Clinton liked dealing with him. "Yeltsin drunk," Clinton once quipped, "is better than most of the alternatives sober."

But even Clinton's patience was tested when Yeltsin visited Washington, D.C., in 1995. Apparently the Russian leader drank the better part of the day, continued on through dinner, and kept at it well into the night. Clinton went to bed sometime before midnight, but in the early morning hours an apologetic Secret Service agent rang him awake with a "problem."

The "problem" was this: a boisterous Boris was out on Pennsylvania Avenue, clad only in his boxers, and drunkenly attempting to flag down a cab. It seems that Boris desired a pizza. When the Russian leader ignored the suggestion that he should go back inside Blair House (his guest quarters for the visit), the agents reluctantly called a bleary-eyed President Clinton.

The Yeltsin incident only came to light when an oral history of Clinton's White House years was published in 2009 (*The Clinton Tapes: Wrestling History with the President* by Taylor Branch). The agents eventually coaxed the belligerent Boris back inside. Clinton later sighed, "Well, he got his pizza."

LAST CALL

More proof that Bill is smart: President Clinton opted to drink red wine—rather than the extremely potent maotai—when toasting with Chinese officials.

OBAMA

★ **2009–2017** ★

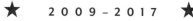

"BUT, THEN AGAIN, THERE'S NEVER A BAD DAY FOR A
BEER AND A WEISSWURST."

—Barack Obama

DEMOCRATIC DRINKING OPS

AT THE RISK OF PROVOKING an elephant charge from the GOP mascot or a swift kick in the face from the Democratic mule, one can argue that Barack Hussein Obama and Ronald Reagan have some similarities, at least when it comes to—for lack of a better phrase—"the drinking photo op."

For example, consider that both Reagan and Obama traveled to Ireland and visited a pub in the respective villages in which some of their ancestors once resided.

In addition, both presidents knew that it doesn't hurt one's image to be seen sipping a beer—the blue-collar man's drink—in relaxed settings such as a barbecue (Ronnie) or while watching a basketball game (Barry).

Of course, as the former governor of California, Reagan prided himself on knowing some fine wines from that state. But Obama, the forty-fourth president, is no stranger to excellent vintages from Napa Valley, either.

In his book *Dreams from My Father*, Obama discusses how alcohol plagued his Kenyan-born father and how his white grandfather would sometimes sneak him into a dive bar in Hawaii when he was ten or eleven. "Gramps" would have a whiskey, and young Barack would settle for a soda and perhaps a chance to smack some billiard balls around on the green felt.

As a teenager, Obama drank alcohol and experimented with drugs. By college, however, Obama became more focused on his academic career.

THE BEER SUMMIT

President Obama had resided in the White House only a few months when he became mired in a national controversy and decided that he might have a way to, if not solve, at least soothe the heated issue.

The solution? In a word, beer.

On July 16, 2009, Cambridge, Massachusetts, police arrested Henry Louis Gates Jr. during a 911 call concerning an alleged break-in at a residence. The residence happened to be where Gates—a black Harvard University professor—lived, and the "break-in" turned out to be him simply trying to get into his own house after returning from a long trip.

The incident became a national story when Obama questioned the validity of the arrest on racial grounds. He later admitted that he had not worded his response in the best way.

In an attempt to bring all parties together for a dialogue, and in an effort to move past the inflammatory incident, the president invited Dr. Gates and Sergeant James Crowley (the arresting officer) to the White House to talk things out over a couple of beers.

The former antagonists, President Obama, and Vice President Joe Biden all gathered near the White House Rose Garden on July 30. Beers were poured (Biden's a "near-beer," as he was a teetotaler), and the meeting entered the historical record forever as "The Beer Summit."

A PUB AND A PRESIDENT

Obama, the son of a white woman (the late Ann Dunham) and a Kenyan student named Barack Obama, traced his ancestry on his mother's side back to Ireland. One Falmouth Kearney, a cobbler, reportedly was the first Irishman on Obama's mother's side to immigrate to the States during the Irish Potato Famine in 1850.

In 2011, President Obama traveled to the Emerald Isle, to a tiny village (with a population of about three hundred) called Moneygall in Offlay County.

As expected, Obama's arrival set the village and surrounding area into a beehive of activity. And since this was Ireland, a sampling of Guinness at the village local pub—in this case the Hayes Pub—was on the agenda.

ADVANCE WORK, INDEED!

We tend to view the Secret Service agents as hardworking, diligent, always-on-alert kind of guys. But it is not always such drudgework, with the occasional dose of danger thrown in. Sometimes the job can be, well, refreshing!

In Moneygall, the Secret Service men checked out the Hayes Pub quite thoroughly—and that meant diligently sampling the beer—before the president and first lady Michelle Obama entered the cozy establishment. In fact, the presidential couple joked about it: "How often has our staff been in here?" smiled Michelle.

"Yeah, how much advance work did they do?" the president chimed in.

BUILDING A PINT

Obama showed his knowledge of Irish pub culture by patiently waiting for the barkeep to "build" his pint of Guinness—which basically means the publican slowly adds more stout to the glass, then lets it rest, then slowly adds some more—the purpose being not to have too much foam in the pour. All this is allegedly in search of the elusive "perfect pint."

"You tell me when it's properly settled," said the president, displaying his knowledge of pub ritual. "I don't want to mess this up!"

WRECKING A PINT

This is where Obama and Reagan diverge. When Reagan visited Ireland, he barely tried one sip of his Guinness, then switched to a red-amber Smithwicks and also failed to finish that. Fair enough; Ronald Reagan never claimed to be a big beer drinker.

AN ISLAND-STYLE SIPPER

As Barack Obama is the first and only president who hails from the islands of Hawaii, it is appropriate to offer up a beverage that might be enjoyed in that state, perhaps poolside. The Hawaiian Punch cocktail is a delicious and refreshing way to toast the forty-fourth president from the fiftieth state.

Hawaiian Punch
1 oz. orange flavored rum
1 oz. raspberry flavored rum
1 oz. vanilla flavored vodka
3 oz. cranberry juice
3 oz. pineapple juice
Maraschino cherry and/or pineapple slice for garnish

Combine all ingredients in a shaker half full of ice cubes. Shake well and strain into a hurricane glass filled with ice cubes. Garnish with a cherry and/or pineapple slice.

> ## The president actually killed his pint!
> ## He gets my vote.

Barack Obama, however, promptly destroyed his pint. He drank a healthy slug of the stout to start off (after some spirited exchanges of the Irish toast "Slainte!" around the pub) and essentially took it down in a half dozen pulls or so. (Michelle also sampled the renowned Dublin-brewed stout, if at a more measured pace.)

As one enthused Irishman who viewed the festivities on television later put it: "The president actually killed his pint! He gets my vote."

Obama admitted that this Guinness was not his first round of stout on Irish soil. The president had savored one at Shannon Airport on a previous trip through Ireland (en route to Afghanistan).

"It tastes better here than it does… in the States," Obama remarked. "What I realized was, is that you guys are—you're keeping all the best stuff here!"

That observation drew lots of laughter, as did Obama's next move: he slapped down some money on the bar and announced: "And by the way… I just want you to know that the president pays his bar tab!"

THE HOMEBREWER IN CHIEF

In 2011, something called "White House Honey Ale" (and "White House Honey Porter" and "White House Honey Blonde") made its first appearance.

The president—using his own money—purchased some home-brewing equipment and the ingredients. Some White House staff members with home-brewing expertise then passed along their knowledge to White House kitchen staffers. Some recipes from a local brew shop were collected and tweaked slightly. The kitchen then brewed up a few tasty beers that suddenly the public had great interest in.

"To be honest, we were surprised that the beer turned out so well, since none of us had brewed beer before," admitted Sam Kass, assistant White House chef, on a whitehouse.gov blog. (There are online videos of Kass and fellow staffer Tafari Campbell going through the brewing process step by step.)

One interesting ingredient is the honey—which comes from a beehive on the South Lawn of the White House, quite close to the first lady's kitchen garden. The honey is primarily enlisted to add smoothness to the brew, rather than to provide sweetness.

THE KICKOFF

White House home brew debuted at a 2011 Super Bowl party at the White House. Since the Packers and Steelers knocked helmets in that one, there were also some supportive beers from Wisconsin and Pottsville, Pennsylvania's famous Yuengling lager (Yuengling lays claim to being the oldest continuous brewery in America). The beers—both White House brewed and invited "guest" beers—were called upon to wash down food from both states, too, such as bratwurst from Wisconsin and potato chips from the Keystone State.

But it did not take long for word to leak out that the White House was brewing its own beer. And then everybody wanted some. The outcry prompted the White House to release the recipes on September 1, 2012. Just a few days beforehand, President Obama had announced: "It will be out soon! I can tell you from firsthand experience it is tasty."

White House beers, however, are hard to come by for Joe Six-Pack. Typical batches (which take nearly a month to make from start to finish) yield fewer than one hundred bottles. The honey ales are more apt to appear on special occasions, such as Super Bowls and St. Patrick's Day.

But special guests can sometimes find one of the much-vaunted brews in their hand, too. When decorated war hero Dakota Meyer visited the White House in 2011, he asked if he could have one of the special beers with Obama. He got his wish.

HAVE BEER, WILL TRAVEL

President Obama has been known to take some of the special White House beer on Air Force One, or—when he ran for reelection in 2012 against Republican Mitt Romney—on his campaign tour bus. Sometimes a lucky citizen was "gifted" a White House brew during these travels.

Obama's opponents were not completely beer-less during the 2012 presidential election. While former Massachusetts governor Romney was not an alcohol drinker due to his Mormon faith, Romney's running mate, Representative Paul Ryan (true to his Wisconsin roots), made mention of his favorite foods—and brews—in his vice-presidential acceptance speech, proudly proclaiming: "My veins run with cheese, bratwurst, a Leine's [Leinenkugel's beer from Chippewa Falls], a little Spotted Cow [a microbrew from Wisconsin], and some Miller."

All of which reminds us: never underestimate the role of beer in politics.

All that said, here are the White House recipes for intrepid home-brewers!

WHITE HOUSE HONEY ALE

2 (3.3 lb.) cans light malt extract
1 lb. light dried malt extract
12 oz. crushed amber crystal malt
8 oz. Biscuit Malt
1 lb. White House Honey
1½ oz. Kent Goldings hop pellets
1½ oz. Fuggles hop pellets
2 tsp. gypsum
1 pkg. Windsor dry ale yeast
¾ c. corn sugar for priming

Directions:

1. In a 12 quart pot, steep the grains in a hop bag in 1½ gallons of sterile water at 155 degrees for half an hour. Remove the grains.

2. Add the 2 cans of the malt extract and the dried extract and bring to a boil.

3. For the first flavoring, add the 1½ oz. Kent Goldings and 2 tsp. of gypsum. Boil for 45 minutes.

4. For the second flavoring, add the 1½ oz. Fuggles hop pellets at the last minute of the boil.

5. Add the honey and boil for 5 more minutes.

6. Add 2 gallons chilled sterile water into the primary fermenter and add the hot wort into it. Top with more water to total 5 gallons. There is no need to strain.

7. Pitch yeast when wort temperature is between 70–80 degrees. Fill airlock halfway with water.

8. Ferment at 68–72 degrees for about seven days.

9. Rack to a secondary fermenter after 5 days and ferment for 14 more days.

10. To bottle, dissolve the corn sugar into 2 pints of boiling water for 15 minutes. Pour the mixture into an empty bottling bucket. Siphon the beer from the fermenter over it. Distribute priming sugar evenly. Siphon into bottles and cap. Let sit for 2 to 3 weeks at 75 degrees.

WHITE HOUSE HONEY PORTER

2 (3.3 lb.) cans light unhopped malt extract
¾ lb. Munich malt (cracked)
1 lb. crystal 20 malt (cracked)
6 oz. black malt (cracked)
3 oz. chocolate malt (cracked)
1 lb. White House Honey
10 HBUs bittering hops
½ oz. Hallertaur Aroma hops
1 pkg. Nottingham dry yeast
¾ c. corn sugar for bottling

Directions:

1. In a 6 quart pot, add grains to 2.25 quarts of 168 degree water. Mix well to bring temp down to 155 degrees. Steep on stovetop at 155 degrees for 45 minutes. Meanwhile, bring 2 gallons of water to 165 degrees in a 12 quart pot.

Place strainer over, then pour and spoon all the grains and liquid in. Rinse with 2 gallons of 165 degree water. Let liquid drain through. Discard the grains and bring the liquid to a boil. Set aside.

2. Add the 2 cans of malt extract and honey into the pot. Stir well.

3. Boil for an hour. Add half of the bittering hops at the 15-minute mark, the other half at 30-minute mark, then the aroma hops at the 60-minute mark.

4. Set aside and let stand for 15 minutes.

5. Place 2 gallons of chilled water into the primary fermenter and add the hot wort into it. Top with more water to total 5 gallons if necessary. Place into an ice bath to cool down to 70–80 degrees.

6. Activate dry yeast in 1 cup of sterilized water at 75–90 degrees for 15 minutes. Pitch yeast into the fermenter. Fill airlock halfway with water. Ferment at room temp (64–68 degrees) for 3–4 days.

7. Siphon over to a secondary glass fermenter for another 4–7 days.

8. To bottle, make a priming syrup on the stove with 1 cup sterile water and ¾ cup priming sugar, bring to a boil for five minutes. Pour the mixture into an empty bottling bucket. Siphon the beer from the fermenter over it. Distribute priming sugar evenly. Siphon into bottles and cap. Let sit for 1–2 weeks at 75 degrees.

THE NIGHT-OWL MARTINI MAN

Although it is well established that Obama enjoys an occasional beer and likes fine wine (plus a margarita once in a while), a 2014 feature in the *New Yorker* ("Going the Distance" by David Remnick) observed that the president drinks an old FDR favorite, too. According to Remnick:

> ...The Obamas have taken to hosting occasional off-the-record dinners in the residence upstairs at the White House. The guests ordinarily include a friendly political figure, a business leader, a journalist. Obama drinks a Martini or two... and he and the First Lady are welcoming, funny, and warm. The dinners start at six. At around ten-thirty at one dinner last spring,

the guests assumed the evening was winding down. But when Obama was asked if they should leave, he laughed and said, "Hey, don't go! I'm a night owl! Have another drink." The party went on past 1 A.M.

FDR would have been proud, both of the offer and the drink of choice.

LAST CALL

American leaders typically expect to be treated—or subjected—to the infamous maotai when they visit China. But Chinese president Xi Jinping brought a surprise "roadie" of the potent sorghum-based liquor to Palm Springs, California, for a 2013 summit. Since Xi opened the bottle especially to toast Obama, one assumes the chief executive at least paid "lip service" to the Chinese liquid equivalent of dragon-fire.

Maotai aside, Obama has not missed out on fine wines. A typical lineup of top vintages was served at a dinner held at Harlem's trendy Red Rooster restaurant (where donors paid thirty thousand dollars to dine with the president prior to the 2012 campaign). A lobster salad was accompanied by a Riesling "semi-dry" (Hermann J. Weiner, 2000) from New York's Finger Lakes region; braised short ribs were coupled with the likes of Ridge Geyserville "Essence" from Sonoma County and Brown Estate "Chaos Theory," a 2009 vintage from the African American–owned winery in Napa Valley.

BIDEN

2021 —

"THAT'S RIGHT, GET A SHOT AND HAVE A BEER."

—Joe Biden

TEETOTAL IRISHMAN

I t may be the only commonality between Joe Biden and Donald Trump, but like his presidential predecessor and rival, Biden is a confirmed teetotaler.

The reasons are strikingly similar. Just as Trump maintains that alcohol played a major role in the destruction of his older brother Fred Trump, Biden is quick to admit that alcohol abuse has caused a lot of damage to members of the Biden clan—both past and present. "Joey" grew up around relatives accurately described as serious drinkers, including a favorite uncle who struggled with bouts of alcoholism. Biden's brother Frank also had major struggles with alcohol, but eventually found sobriety.

In an effort to short-circuit what Biden viewed as something of a family curse, he emphatically cautioned his siblings, and later his children, to completely avoid Demon Alcohol. But most of them eventually drank, some in moderation, while others—most notably his son Hunter—tumbled into the abyss of addiction.

"I'm the only Irishman you have met that's never had a drink."

Nevertheless, even in administrations that lean toward temperance, alcohol is never far from the grind of the political process. So there are still stories to be told concerning booze and the Biden administration, even if drinking alcohol has been sidelined to some degree.

RAIL CAR ONE ALE

Although Biden is likely to order up a Coca-Cola when a celebration is on tap, that doesn't mean others can't indulge in something that packs more of a presidential punch.

It was wins in toss-up states like Pennsylvania, Arizona, Michigan, Wisconsin, and Georgia that allowed Biden to prevail in the 2020 presidential election, but it was Biden's diminutive home state of Delaware that charged forth to brew up a beverage worthy of the occasion.

More specifically, it was the Wilmington Brew Works that rose to the challenge. And the brewery did not just produce any basic beer and slap a ho-hum logo on it, but arguably barreled up some suds with some substance and artful design behind the brew.

Thus the debut of Rail Car One, a hearty Northeast India Pale Ale (IPA), on December 7, 2020. The Rail Car One name was a nod to Joe Biden's Wilmington-to-Washington commute—which he undertook for decades and which eventually earned him the nickname of "Amtrak Joe" from media mainstays such as CNN and the *New York Times.* The IPA—no lightweight at 8 percent ABV and featuring three different kinds of hops—immediately sold out.

Wilmington Brew Works vice president of creative and brand marketing John Fusco was quoted in a *Delaware Today* online story: "Joe Biden famously doesn't drink alcohol, and I didn't think it was fair to him to put his likeness on a can. I also enjoyed the challenge of recreating a WPA-era train-style poster."

Also on the can was this claim: "While #46 may not engage in the occasional tipple, his fine friends in The First State certainly do. And that's something we can all agree on." In addition, aviator sunglasses like the ones Biden often wears are on the label. The number of the train on the can—0046—is a nod to Biden's being elected the forty-sixth POTUS.

The brew was purposely released on December 7, Delaware Day, which celebrates the landmark day in 1787 when Delaware became the first state to ratify the Constitution—and thereby the first state in the Union.

President Biden has announced that he is running for a second term; he is the likely Democrat nominee for 2024. One can only hope that Wilmington Brew Works will respond with the obvious: a Rail Car Two ale that runs strong on taste and art, just like its creative predecessor.

IRISH JOE AND HIS DRINKING DOPPELGANGER

Always proud of his Irish bloodlines, Joe Biden has visited the Emerald Isle several times in his life. When he hops across the pond, Biden often stops in Ballina—a picturesque town (population hovering around ten thousand) perched on the River Moy, County Mayo. Scranton Joe traces his Celtic roots to the Blewitt family there—the story being that Biden's great-great-grandfather Edward Blewitt, a local brick manufacturer, sold bricks for the construction of St. Muredach's Cathedral there to pay for his passage to America around 1850. The incentive was to escape the Great Famine caused by the potato blight.

Biden has long made efforts to establish ties with his Irish ancestors. In fact, Biden hosted some of his Blewitt relatives (who still reside in Ballina) at the White House for St. Patrick's Day in 2023. And while President Biden was observing St. Patrick's Day, he tellingly joked, "I'm the only Irishman you have met that's never had a drink."

Apparently, President Biden proved no more flexible on that point when he visited Belfast, Northern Ireland, as well as the Republic of Ireland, in April of 2023. He mainly travelled there to pay homage to the twenty-fifth anniversary of the Good Friday accord, an American-brokered agreement that played a major role in ending decades of bloody sectarian strife in Northern Ireland.

Biden also took the opportunity to visit several spots in Ireland that have personal connections to his ancestral tree. Biden generates considerable buzz in Ballina's pubs for a man most reluctant to hoist a pint of Guinness (unlike his former boss, President

Obama, when he appeared at Hayes's Pub in Moneygall, his mother's ancestral home in Ireland).

First and foremost, there is Harrison's Pub. One would be hard-pressed to meet a bigger Biden fan than Harrison's publican Derek Leonard. He hosted Biden at his pub in 2016 and had his photo snapped with then VP Biden in front of his establishment. That picture is now proudly displayed inside Harrison's. In 2020, in celebration of Biden's election, the pub's windows featured Biden-Harris campaign posters, and American flags were flying from the roof.

Not to be outdone, Paddy Mac's—another Ballina pub—was harboring a Joe Biden look-alike, a local fella whose real name is Anthony "Bosley" Timoney. According to an online Galway publication, Mr. Timoney—an aging Irish bachelor with some similarities to Biden in appearance, including a presidential-looking suit and some cool shades—was up for meeting the forty-sixth president. "I'm a big fan of Joe," Timoney said a few days before Biden's expected arrival. "I might go for a pint with him. I'll be round next week. I'd like to meet him."[1]

Perhaps Timoney did not get the word; Biden is rather unlikely to become his drinking buddy—well, anyway, as least not in the true sense of what that means in Ireland. And while his meeting with the actual president was up in the air, Timoney allowed that he was open to celebratory pints and selfies with patrons and/or visitors to Paddy Mac's while all the Biden-in-Ballina hoopla lasted.

DR. JILL CAN CHILL

Dr. Jill Biden is the oldest First Lady to ever reside in the White House (she turned seventy back in 2021), but she'd arguably rank fairly high on the "fun" list compared to many of her younger predecessors. If the forty-sixth POTUS avoids alcohol, Dr. Jill,

---

[1] Michelle Fleming, "Joe Biden's 'Twin' Spotted outside Popular Irish Pub as Photos Show US President's Lookalike," GalwayBeo, April 8, 2023, https://www.galwaybeo.ie/news/ireland-news/joe-bidens-twin-spotted-outside-8335853.

by contrast, is never hesitant to enjoy a glass of red wine while preparing dinner at home or dining out at a popular bistro, or to wash down a soft pretzel at a Philadelphia Phillies baseball game with a beer.

And it is traditional for wine to be an important part of entertaining foreign dignitaries when there are state dinners at the White House. President Biden, of course, rolls with something non-alcoholic, but the First Lady is willing to imbibe at moderate levels.

A visit from French president Emmanuel Macron and his wife Brigitte in early December 2022 was the occasion for an interesting toast. Approximately three hundred people hobnobbed under an outdoor pavilion tent on the South Lawn at the black-tie event. Of course, given that this was a visit from the French, there *had* to be an offering of high-quality wine.

But what *kind* of wine perhaps took a little bit of thought. The result was something that might have brought a smile to the face of the Marquis de Lafayette himself—there was a trio of California wines, but the wines all had some kind of French connection:

- Roederer Estate Brut Rosé, produced in Mendocino County by the French Champagne house that began making wine there in the 1980s
- Newton Unfiltered Napa Valley Chardonnay, owned by the French luxury firm LMVH, rebounding after 2020 wildfires destroyed much of its cellar
- Anakota Knights Valley Cabernet Sauvignon, owned by Jackson Family Wines but crafted by their business partner, Bordeaux winemaker Pierre Seillan

What better way to honor the historic ties between the French and the Americans?

The wines did not suffer in their presentation; they were served in elegant Baccarat crystal. One assumes the wines aptly complemented the scrumptious dinner of poached Maine lobster (with American caviar), beef with shallot marmalade, and an orange chiffon cake for dessert, among other culinary enticements.

But back to the toast . . . well, actually *two* toasts.

The first was the "official" state dinner toast. President Biden exclaimed: "Vive la France and God bless America!"

The French president responded in kind: "Long live the United States of America, long live France, and long live the friendship between our two countries!"

The guests all dutifully clinked their glasses.

But the second toast was one that took place at the dinner table and was witnessed by only a dozen or so people. Dr. Jill Biden happened to mention that she embraced an exercise routine that energized her when enduring the rigors of the campaign trail. President Macron immediately asked if she was "ready" for the 2024 campaign trail, and Dr. Biden affirmed that she was. Whereupon Macron rose to toast this exchange with a glass of wine and President Joe Biden toasted too—albeit with a glass of Coca-Cola.

BIDEN'S "BEER BRIBE"

When COVID vaccination rates began to slow in 2021, President Joe Biden found an unlikely ally in his push for Americans to line up to get the shot: beer.

The project was spearheaded by Anheuser-Busch, as the brewing giant offered to pony up a free beer to any American of legal drinking age willing to get the COVID-19 shot over the July Fourth holiday.

And America's non-drinking chief executive was almost giddy about the idea, as he hoped to coax the nation to an elusive 70 percent vaccination rate.

"That's right, get a shot and have a beer," President Biden announced in early June 2021. "Free beer for everyone 21 years or over to celebrate the independence from the virus."[2]

2 "Remarks by President Biden on the COVID-19 Response and Vaccination Program," The White House, June 2, 2021, https://www.whitehouse.gov/briefing-room/speeches-remarks/2021/06/02/remarks-by-president-biden-on-the-covid-19-response-and-vaccination-program/.

KAMALA HARRIS AND
THE COCKTAIL KICKOFF

When Kamala Harris was announced as President Biden's running mate in 2020, some mixologists promptly responded with drink recipes to honor the historic moment of a woman of color landing on a presidential ticket. (Something that did not happen for Mike Pence in 2016.)

Two such cocktails, adapted from originals featured in *Forbes* magazine, appear here. The Biden/Harris Ticket was created by Bay Area mixologists Janice Bailon and Simone Mims, who included the St. George craft liqueurs in a shout-out to a local business in Kamala Harris's Northern California. The Kamala Harris was created by New York City's Estelle Bossy.

The Biden/Harris Ticket

2 oz. bourbon
½ oz. St. George Spiced Pear
¼ oz. St. George Coffee Liqueur
pinch of brown sugar
1 oz. dark chocolate
1 T sea salt

Grate the chocolate, add the salt, stir together, and spread the mixture out on a small plate.

Rim a cocktail glass with one of the liqueurs and press it upside down into the chocolate-salt mixture. Pour the bourbon and the remaining liqueurs into a different glass and add the brown sugar. Stir until the sugar dissolves. Add ice and stir a few times gently. Pour the cocktail into the rimmed glass and serve.

Kamala Harris

1 oz. Pomp & Whimsy Gin Liqueur
¾ oz. dry vermouth
¾ oz. lemon cordial (Bickfords or El Guapo are good choices)
5 thick slices of cucumber
3 oz. Champagne

Pour Pomp & Whimsy, vermouth, and lemon cordial into a cocktail shaker. Add 2 cucumber slices. Fill to the top with ice and shake vigorously. Double strain into a chilled cocktail glass. Top with Champagne. Garnish with remaining cucumber slices and a large chunk of ice.

"As people get back together with friends and family for Independence Day, we are celebrating the progress we've made together the best way we know how—over a beer—and are delivering on our promise of beer for America," confirmed Michel Doukeris, the chief executive of Anheuser-Busch.[3]

Speaking on CNN, even FDA vaccine advisory committee member Dr. Paul Offit had to smile at the strategy of a sudsy enticement.

"I think it will help," said Offit. "I think for those people who need a nudge this provides that nudge, although you'd think enough of an incentive would be offered by having to avoid being hospitalized or killed by this virus. But if beer works, I'm all for it."[4]

3 "Budweiser Partners with Actor Bill Pullman to Recreate Iconic Presidential Speech from Independence Day: 'Go Fourth, America,'" Anheuser-Busch, June 30, 2021, https://www.anheuser-busch.com/newsroom/budweiser-recreates-iconic-speech-from-independence-day-go-fourth-america.
4 "CNN NEWSROOM: Florida Governor Bans Transgender Females From Sports; President Biden Declares June Month of Action For COVID Shots; Trump Telling People He Will Be Reinstated as President?; Infrastructure Negotiations. Aired 3-3:30p ET" (transcript), CNN, June 2, 2021, http://www.cnn.com/TRANSCRIPTS/2106/02/cnr.09.html.

LAST CALL ....

Hunter Biden detailed his alcohol abuse in his memoir *Beautiful Things*. Hunter said he had first knocked back a glass of Champagne at age eight and that his drinking has continued to get worse (and eventually led to habitual drug abuse) through his adult years: "I've been so desperate for a drink that I couldn't make the one-block walk between a liquor store and my apartment without uncapping the bottle to take a swig. . . ."[5]

Saturday Night Live's Maya Rudolph depicted Kamala Harris several times, including as the "cool aunt"—wearing hip-looking shades and clutching a frozen drink in her hand (complete with one of those tiny "drink umbrellas").

Speaking of "cool" . . . if you want to keep your beer cold with a sleeve (a "coozie"), you can get one online that features Joe Biden's image with one of his more bristling catchphrases: "Shut up, man!" It probably works on soda cans as well. (The anti-Biden camp offer numerous beer sleeve alternatives that are less than flattering to JB.)

In the crucial swing state of Wisconsin, brewer Kirk Bangstad did not hesitate to let his patrons and neighbors know where he stood in the 2020 election. He put a sign outside his Minocqua Brewing Company that read, "Biden for President." When Biden won, Bangstad put out a Kölsch-style beer to commemorate the moment, one that he felt reflected the personality of the forty-sixth POTUS: "inoffensive and not too bitter."

---

5 Hunter Biden, *Beautiful Things: A Memoir* (New York: Gallery Books, 2021).

LIST OF COCKTAILS

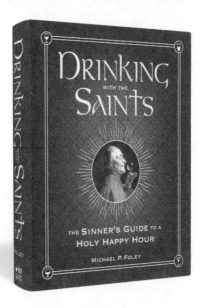

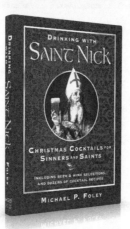

FROM THE OTHER SIDE OF THE AISLE...

Do you have friends who are Republicans? Or bipartisan? Or do you want a matched set? If so, then get the counterpart to the book you're holding in your hand—it's called *Drinking with the Republicans: The Politically Incorrect History of Conservative Concoctions*. Just like this book, it's chock-full of anecdotes about presidential drinking, plus incudes twenty-eight cocktail recipes hand-picked for each president.

AVAILABLE WHEREVER BOOKS ARE SOLD!